INTERSTELLAR FLIGHT MAGAZINE BEST OF YEAR ONE

ERIN BECKER ANDREA BLYTHE JEREMY BRETT

CASSANDRA ROSE CLARKE KAYLEE CRAIG

MICHAEL GLAZNER PIPER J. DANIELS

ARCHITA MITTRA J.T. MORSE AIMEE OGDEN

CAITLIN STARLING JOHN TUTTLE E.D. WALKER

T.D. WALKER HOLLY LYN WALRATH KADE WALTON

INTERSTELLAR FLIGHT MAGAZINE BEST OF YEAR ONE

INTERSTELLAR FLIGHT PRESS BEST OF YEAR ONE

Cover Illustration by amdandy

Edited by Holly Lyn Walrath, Cassandra Rose Clarke, Michael Glazner, and Kade Walton

Published by Interstellar Flight Press, Houston, Texas.

www.interstellarflightpress.com

ISBN (eBook): 978-1-7338862-7-7

ISBN (paperback): 978-1-7338862-6-0

ISBN (hardcover): 978-1-7338862-8-4

First Edition: August 2020

CONTENTS

1 / THE ONES WHO WALK AWAY

URSULA K. LE GUIN'S MOST FAMOUS SHORT STORY IS JUST AS RELEVANT AS IT WAS IN 1973

By Holly Lyn Walrath

The people at the door never say anything, but the child, who has not always lived in the tool room, and can remember sunlight and its mother's voice, sometimes speaks. "I will be good," it says. "Please let me out. I will be good!" They never answer. The child used to scream for help at night, and cry a good deal, but now it only makes a kind of whining, "eh-haa, eh-haa," and it speaks less and less often.

- URSULA K. LE GUIN, "THE ONES WHO WALK AWAY FROM OMELAS"

Ursula K. Le Guin's most famous short story was first published in October 1973 in *New Dimensions* 3, a hardcover anthology edited by Robert Silverberg. It won the 1974 Hugo Award for Best Short Story. In the years since, "The Ones Who Walk Away from Omelas" has been taught in classrooms across the globe and anthologized many times. Similar to stories like Shirley Jackson's "The Lottery" (*The New Yorker*, 1948), Charlotte Perkins Gilman's "The Yellow Wallpaper" (*The New England Magazine,* 1892), or Hans Christian Anderson's "The Little Match Girl" (1845), it is further proof that shorter works carry just as powerful a legacy as longer ones.

"The Ones Who Walk Away from Omelas" tells the fictional story of a city where everyone is happy—but that happiness is contingent on a very dark secret. In response to Fyodor Dostoevsky's *The Brothers Karamazov,* and William James' "The Moral Philosopher and the Moral Life," Omelas explores a city in which everyone is happy, mature, intelligent, passionate, and decidedly not wretched. War does not exist, there are few rules and laws, and no discernable government.

In short, Omelas is the Utopia you've always envisioned.

One of my favorite lines, as Le Guin explains this, is when she asserts, "The trouble is, we have a bad habit, encouraged by pedants and sophisticates, of considering happiness as something rather stupid. Only pain is intellectual, only evil interesting. This is the treason of the artist: a refusal to admit the banality of evil and the terrible boredom of pain." Le Guin explores the binary war between happiness and pain, and how as humans, we tend to place these emotions into neat categories, ignoring the gray areas between.

But all is not perfect in paradise. The cost of the populace's happiness is pain. The pain of one child, to be precise. The citizens of Omelas know of this child, wasting away, forgotten, pushed aside. And yet they choose happiness. We're presented with this binary over and over again in pop culture: Isn't the pain of the few worth the happiness of the many? It's the question asked by Spock in Star Trek's *The Wrath of Khan*, "Logic clearly dictates that the needs of the many outweigh the needs of the few."

As the story closes, it speaks of those "who walk away from Omelas." These select few are presented as the wiser because they chose to leave and find a new world, one that is "a place even less imaginable to most of us than the city of happiness . . . It is possible that it does not exist."

So this is the binary Le Guin's story gives us. Do we stay in paradise, always knowing it would be a little bit imperfect, or do we leave?

Like the citizens of Omelas, modern humanity feels more comfortable sitting in our safety, unwilling to see the price for our happiness. Because acknowledging the problem means more than posting on social media or writing our representatives. It means changing *ourselves*.

A FABLE FOR THE AGES

In 2018, I was honored to serve on a panel at Readercon in remembrance of Ursula K. Le Guin. I was there to talk about her poetry, but I came away with a keen sense of the impact of her career. An editor of a popular SFF publication spoke of how she receives a response story to "The Ones Who Walk Away from Omelas" at least once a month. It has been called a story that defies genre, an allegory of privilege, a hideous bargain, and a cautionary tale.

Le Guin said of Omelas in *The Unreal and the Real*, ". . . [its] a fable, I think . . . it has had a long and happy career of being used by teachers to upset students and make them argue fiercely about morality."

One of the panelists asked of the story, "It makes us wonder, what would we do if we had to make that choice?"

My response was, "We are already making that choice, right now."

Or, as Margaret Atwood would put it: "Where in the world [can] we find a society in which the happiness of some does not depend on the misery of others? How do we build Omelas, minus the tortured child?" ("Margaret Atwood: We Lost Ursula K. Le Guin When We Needed Her Most," *The Washington Post,* Jan 24, 2018). When we are living in a world where most people are happy at the expense of the few, it is hard to imagine a new reality. Hard times are *here*, and it's not so difficult to see who profits the most.

On Christmas Day 2018, an eight-year-old boy from Guatemala died in United States custody, the second death of a child at the U.S.-Mexico border in three weeks ("8-Year-Old Migrant Child From Guatemala Dies in U.S. Custody," *The New York Times,* December 25, 2018.) As of the publication of this anthology, that number has risen to six. In detention facilities, children sleep on mats with a single blanket. Colds, fevers, and other illnesses are rampant. On both sides of the political divide, politicians push blame away. President Trump blamed Democrats for "pathetic immigration policies" ("Trump Politicizes Deaths of Two Immigrant Children to Score Points in Border Wall Fight," *The Washington Post,* December 29, 2018). We are told that children suffer because it keeps the rest of us safe. Meanwhile, Democrats shook their heads and called the death a horrific tragedy.

My spouse is a pediatric physical therapist at one of the best hospitals in the nation. Every day he deals with insurance denying coverage to children who need heart transplants. He sees parents separated from their children because they don't have the resources to care for them. He knows the cost and burden of a child's pain. As he counsels young therapists in how to deal with emotional burnout, he's often repeated the words: "You just deal with it and move on." You let yourself feel, but at the end of the day, there's always another child that needs your help. There is no choice to walk away.

I could fill this essay with examples until it's a novel in itself.

Everyone seems to agree that things are broken. In our current society, it's easy to feel like there are only two choices.

And indeed, that seems to be the primary response to Le Guin's work—that the ones who walk away from the issue have, in some way, chosen the best route. That the only solution to a broken place is to leave it in the dust.

HOW DO WE MAKE THE THIRD CHOICE?

But when we give in to that kind of polarized thought, we lose sight of the real victims. Maybe there's another way. Maybe we can choose to stay and fix the problems at hand. As the brilliant author N.K. Jemisin puts it:

> *". . . you've got to fix it, especially when there's nowhere to walk away to. You go anywhere else in our current world and you're either being completely exploited by capitalism or somewhat exploited by capitalism. So, I mean, it's just a question of what kind of suffering you want to put yourself through."*
>
> *- "A TRUE UTOPIA: AN INTERVIEW WITH N. K. JEMISIN," THE PARIS REVIEW, DECEMBER 3, 2018.)*

(Even Jemisin herself wrote an Omelas response story, "The Ones Who Stay and Fight," available in her collection *How Long 'til Black Future Month?* (Orbit, 2018))

Literature as an art form has a unique power. For me, reading Omelas reminds me to think outside of the box. It helps me to process Le Guin's thought experiment through the lens of today's news. The fact that the story has captivated readers for so many years speaks to its broad nature, its ability to transcend not just one social issue, but many.

But words do not exist in a vacuum. As Le Guin said, "Words do have power. Names have power. Words are events; they do things, change things. They transform both speaker and hearer; they feed energy back and forth and amplify it" (*The Wave in the Mind: Talks and Essays on the Writer, the Reader, and the Imagination* (Penguin Random House, 2004)). A conversation cannot be one-sided. This is the power of literature —to become more than words on a page and enter into a conversation with the reader. It asks, *what would you do, dear reader?*

After Ursula K. Le Guin's death, we need her work more than ever. We need *art* more than ever. To the writers, artists, creators, and dreamers: I encourage you to read "The Ones Who Walk Away from Omelas." I encourage you to respond, to imagine new worlds, and to think not in terms of one choice, but many. As Le Guin said, we need writers who can remember freedom.

> *We live in capitalism, its power seems inescapable—but then, so did the divine right of kings. Any human power can be resisted and changed by human beings. Resistance and change often begin in art. Very often in our art, the art of words.*
>
> *- URSULA K. LE GUIN, NATIONAL BOOK AWARDS SPEECH, 2014*

2 / *MONSTERS UNDER THE BED (AND OUTSIDE THE WINDOW)*

AN INTERVIEW WITH T. KINGFISHER, AUTHOR OF THE TWISTED ONES

by E.D. Walker

I take things that I'm scared of . . . and then I write that into the book. If other people are scared of it too, then I'm not alone.

- T. KINGFISHER

T. Kingfisher is the pen name of Hugo Award-winning author Ursula Vernon. As T. Kingfisher, she's known for fantasy novels with kind and practical protagonists. While her books usually contain some elements of horror, *The Twisted Ones* (Gallery/Saga Press, 2019) is her first horror novel.

Interstellar Flight Press: Your previous adult books have been fantasy novels (usually with some horror elements creeping in). Was writing a full-on horror novel like *The Twisted Ones* a different experience for you? Did you encounter any challenges writing *The Twisted Ones* that you didn't have with your fantasy works?

T. KINGFISHER: I did! The problem with writing anything contemporary is . . . well . . . cell phones and the Internet. You have to find a reason that the heroine can't just call 911 or look up the answer to her problems. Fortunately, there's still a lot of spots in rural NC with very spotty cell coverage.

IFP: *The Twisted Ones* is loosely based on an old story by Arthur Machen that provides the inspiration in your novel for "The Green Book," a notebook which kicks off part of the plot of *The Twisted Ones*. What made you want to build a story around Machen's work? Did using his book as a jumping-off point cause you any problems?

TK: To a certain extent, the book was inspired by my long-standing problem with found manuscript stories. Machen's "The White People" (1904) is probably the ur-Found Manuscript—it's all this long, strange narrative that wanders between dreamlike and "Dear God, I want a copyeditor." Some gorgeous turns of phrase, but a lot of . . . stuff. So the story [in *The Twisted Ones*] became partly about an editor reacting to this strange rambling manuscript that's both creepy and just very strangely written. But the line about the twisted ones is one of the most beautiful and weird in the book, and I used it as a jumping-off point to get into the strange happenings in the woods.

> *Then I made faces like the faces on the rocks, and I twisted myself about like the twisted ones, and I lay down flat on the ground like the dead ones, and I went up to one that was grinning, and put my arms round him and hugged him.*
>
> *- ARTHUR MACHEN, "THE WHITE PEOPLE" (1904)*

IFP: I believe I saw somewhere that you've mentioned writing a horror novel as being an ambition of yours for a long time. Do you have any horror authors who inspired you?

TK: Oh goodness! Lots, more than I could probably fit in one page, and probably which are familiar to nearly every other writer out there. But one of my great inspirations that doesn't get mentioned a lot is the SCP website [hosted on a collaborative, community-based wiki], which is this wonderful sprawling shared universe, where a government agency is trying to contain all these horrible paranormal things. Some of the most creepy, effective writing I've ever read has been from there.

IFP: Are you planning to continue writing adult horror for the foreseeable future?

TK: I definitely think I'll be writing more horror—well, I mean, I already sold another novel, so that's a good sign!—but I'd definitely like to write more after that. I get told that my fantasy has a lot of horror elements, so I suspect I don't have much choice.

IFP: I wanted to mention Bongo, the heroine's dog in the book. He was one of my favorite parts and often provided heart and humor during some of the darkest moments of *The Twisted Ones*. Was he always a character in the book? Or did you add him later? Is he based on one of your own dogs?

TK: He was always a character, right from the beginning. I didn't quite know what I was going to do with him, but a friendly animal companion is a recurring theme in my books. I do own a pair of coonhounds, and he's pretty solidly based on one of them. They are lovely dogs, good-natured, not particularly bright, and absolutely single-minded once they get on a scent.

IFP: I have to tell you, *The Twisted Ones* scared the hell out of me.

TK: Oh man, I never know whether to gloat or apologize when people say that!

Thank you and I'm sorry?

IFP: How did you craft the horror elements when you were writing this? Did you manage to freak yourself out while writing the creepy stuff, or are you immune to your own scary writing by now?

TK: Ah . . . I'm not exactly immune, but writing it helps immunize me, if that makes any sense. I take things that I'm scared of—I have a longstanding nervousness of looking out windows in the dark, in case there's something pressed against them, for example—and then I write that into the book. If other people are scared of it too, then I'm not alone!

Once I've written it, I am sometimes less frightened of it myself. Not in this one, so much . . . there's too many potential things outside the window . . . but I once did a comic about a monster under the bed, and afterwards, I wasn't as frightened of things grabbing my ankles in the dark, because I had created a heroic dustbunny patrolling the underside of the bed, and I knew he was on the case.

Generally, though, I think horror authors are scared of a lot of things. We just know that misery loves company.

IFP: You just released a charming fantasy novella called *Minor Mage* (Red Wombat Studio, 2019) about a preteen magician trying to save his town from a drought. What's up next for you after that? Do you have any more self-published works close to completion?

TK: I do! A longer book called *Paladin's Grace* should be coming out for the holidays, assuming all the ducks line themselves into a row. And I've got three or four books in various stages of completion at two different publishers, so there's a lot more to come!

T. Kingfisher is the vaguely absurd pen-name of Ursula Vernon. In another life, she writes children's books and weird comics and has won the Hugo, Sequoyah, and Ursa Major awards, as well as a half-dozen Junior Library Guild selections. In addition to her writing, T. Kingfisher is an artist, a gardener, and the owner of a collection of cats, hound dogs, and incorrigible chickens. The Twisted Ones *is available wherever books are sold.*

3 / *THE GREATEST ARSENAL: SCIENCE FICTION LIBRARIES AND ARCHIVES*

HOW SFF LIBRARIANS AND ARCHIVISTS ARE SAVING THE PAST FOR THE FUTURE'S RESEARCHERS

by Jeremy Brett

> *"You want weapons? We're in a library. Books are the best weapon in the world. This room's the greatest arsenal we could have. Arm yourself!"*
>
> - THE DOCTOR, "TOOTH AND CLAW" (*DOCTOR WHO*, SERIES 2, EPISODE 2, 2006)

Science fiction and fantasy fans are no strangers to the imaginative power of the *Library* (or the *Archives*). There's something perennially entrancing about the concept of a limitless repository of information that spans vast eras of history (as with Jorge Luis Borges' Library of Babel (1962), Isaac Asimov's "Encyclopedia Galactica" from his *Foundation* trilogy, or the library assembled from across time and space by the Great Race of Yith in Lovecraft's "The Shadow Out of Time"(*Astounding Stories*, 1936)). Equally compelling are the many libraries of fantasy, in which mysterious volumes of magic and sorcery are locked away on endless shelves, to be examined at the reader's peril. We all know well and love the library at Unseen University in Terry Pratchett's *Discworld* Series, presided over by the man-turned-orangutan Librarian; the library of Morpheus in Neil Gaiman's comic series *The Sandman* (which contains, among other things, books that only exist in the dreams of their authors); and the fifty-two levels of the Great Library from the *Thursday Next* series by Jasper Fforde, in which every book that has been written or will ever be written resides.

Libraries and archives also serve in science fiction and fantasy as sites that preserve—either by design or accident—the last remnants of lost civilizations, such as the collection of pre-World War III relics maintained (and misinterpreted) by the Albertian Order of Leibowitz in Walter Miller's novel *A Canticle for Leibowitz* (1959), or the small assemblage of disintegrating books that instantly turn to dust at Rod Taylor's touch in the 1960 film *The Time Machine*. Whatever narrative or function these institutions might serve, the idea of vast repositories of knowledge—whether restricted to a small group of elites, or available to all—is an enthralling one.

Therefore, it makes perfect sense that in the real world we look to libraries and archives to protect and preserve the history of the genre itself, carrying on the mission of their fictional counterparts. There exists a small but growing number of institutions (the majority of them in the United States) that collect materials that document, chart, and explain the history and development of science fiction and fantasy as a genre. These materials include books (novels, anthologies, collections), scholarly journals, comic books, magazines, art, ephemera, objects, audiovisual materials such as film, record albums, or audiocassettes, fanworks such as fanzines and vids, as well as archival collections that include manuscripts and correspondence from genre creators and associates. The variety of materials in any one repository rivals that of the universe itself. (Well, maybe one of the smaller universes.)

Major institutions that systematically collect SFF materials include, to name some of the most prominent: the Eaton Collection of Science Fiction and Fantasy at the University of California, Riverside (the world's largest academic SFF collection); the Merrill Collection of Science Fiction, Speculation and Fantasy at the Toronto Public Library (the largest in Canada); the Science Fiction Foundation Archive at the University of Liverpool (the largest in Europe); the SFWA Collection at Northern Illinois University, University of Kansas (with its storied James Gunn Center for Science Fiction); Syracuse University; the University of Iowa; and the Browne Popular Culture Library at Bowling Green State University.

Science Fiction and Fantasy merit serious study and, as with any form of literature or art or science, require the primary sources for research that libraries and archives provide.

The existence of collections like these is significant for the SFF genres for several reasons. They preserve the story of What Came Before (or in many cases, What Is Going On Right Now) in science fiction and fantasy for future generations of readers, fans, and scholars. That's especially important because both the published and the historical record in documents of SFF have so many hidden histories within them that deserve exposure and attention. The old, traditional story of SFF is one told by and for cisgender white men.

However, using the vast array of historical materials that our great arsenals preserve, we can rediscover and bring back to the light the work of women, LGBTQ creators, the non-white creators, and others who have always been part of the story but whose contributions did not always go recognized or fully appreciated. And independent of the nature of the creator, these arks of history preserve books and stories and articles and all sorts of other works by obscure creators that may deserve a new look. (Think of the decades worth of stories in pulp magazines that can still inspire joy, excitement, and escapism but were never anthologized or collected anywhere, for example.)

Through conscious efforts, these arsenals can help ensure that the current state of SFF is reflected in the documentary record, too. Curators, librarians, and archivists can collect the works and the papers of newer, rising, or less-established creators and make sure that the history of this generation of SFF creators is preserved alongside the records of the traditional canon.

Finally, the existence of these collections in major academic or public institutions have a deeper meaning. They signify that science fiction and fantasy are not only frivolous bits of popular culture that don't count as "real" literature (or film, or whatever else); in fact, they are genres as worthy as any of scholarly attention and research, and of the time and energy of students. Science Fiction and Fantasy merit serious study and, as with any form of literature or art or science, require the primary sources for research that libraries and archives provide. (In conjunction with this, note that several institutions offer Science Fiction Studies as an accepted minor or other program of study: these include UC-Riverside's *Speculative Fiction and Cultures of Science* program, the Science Fiction Studies minor program at Georgia Tech, and the new Science Fiction concentration in Texas A&M University's Department of English.)

These collections are also physical manifestations of the belief that the materials therein have lasting significance because the genre as a whole has a genuine and real impact on society and culture, on literature, on gender studies, on sociology, and even on science and engineering fields. As we all know, SFF inspires, enlightens, entertains, frightens, and causes us to question why things are and how things could be. That kind of impact demands respect, time, and attention.

As an example of what these arsenals can hold, I can speak most directly to the collection that I curate, the Science Fiction & Fantasy Research Collection at Cushing Memorial Library & Archives, Texas A&M University. Our collection traces its origins back to the mid-1970s, when librarian Hal Hall (a noted SF scholar and bibliographer in his own right) acquired for Cushing two hundred old SF paperbacks and convinced the director that, indeed, science fiction was a subject whose history merited preservation alongside Cushing's existing collections relating to military history, the history of Texas, the history of books and printing, and other important subjects. From that small seed has grown over the succeeding decades one of the largest collections—one of the strongest arsenals—of its kind in the world.

The collection at Cushing is comprised of thousands upon thousands of items, including books, magazines, scholarly journals, pulp magazines, three-dimensional objects, items of ephemera, audiovisual materials, and archival collections that together chart the course of science fiction and fantasy since the seventeenth century (one of the oldest items in the collection is the 1640 work *A discourse concerning a new world & another planet* by John Wilkins).

The collection is vast, incorporating centuries of published works. Part of the collection's mission is to capture works, both important and less remembered, from the long history of science fiction and fantasy. Items range from the 1823 second edition of *Frankenstein* (the first to credit Mary Shelley as the author), to a complete run of the famed Ace Doubles (1952–1978), to first editions of Verne and Wells and nearly every other SFF author of note, to the personal SF library that belonged to Anne McCaffrey, to examples of American comic books and Japanese manga, to complete runs of pulps like *Amazing, Astounding*, and *Galaxy*, to collections of genre poetry.

Cushing's arsenal also includes over one hundred individual archival collections, that is, collections of primary documents assembled by creators that include manuscripts, correspondence, drafts, and other materials, that as a whole, document one's life and career. These kinds of things are particularly important because not only is it inherently cool to look at the thing that eventually became the thing we love, but because it lets fans and researchers alike observe how texts evolve from idea to completion and the process surrounding the production of texts. They also provide insights into the minds and sometimes even the whimsies of the creators.

The Collection's largest and most well-known collection is that of fantasy author George R.R. Martin, which encompasses hundreds of boxes of paper records as well as books, objects, and *Game of Thrones*-related merchandise. However, Cushing also holds smaller collections from major figures in the field, such as Arthur C. Clarke, Ray Bradbury, Avram Davidson, Robert Heinlein, Anne McCaffrey, Andre Norton, John Sladek, and Robert Silverberg. In addition, we have a very large collection of archival materials from Michael Moorcock.

As a Texas institution, one of our primary goals is also to chronicle the rich SFF tradition in our state and in the Southwest region generally. To that end, we also have collections of archival materials from locals (or regionals) like Steven Gould, Laura Mixon, Elizabeth Moon, Joe R. Lansdale, Ardath Mayhar, Howard Waldrop, D.L. Young, and our own local literary celebrity Martha Wells.

As I noted above, these arsenals also exist in order to preserve the current state of the field and to make sure that creators from marginalized or overlooked populations are included (as women and minorities are achieving such immense things in the genre today). To that end, working with the authors themselves, I have made an effort for Cushing to become the repository for the archives of newer writers like Marie Brennan, Beth Cato, J. Kathleen Cheney, Brenda Cooper, Alyx Dellamonica, Jeannine Hall Gailey, Stina Leicht, Silvia Moreno-Garcia, Ada Palmer, Kelly Robson, and Django Wexler. One of my goals has been to expand our holdings—both published works and archives—to include more works by writers of color, women writers, LGBTQ writers, and so forth.

A well-stocked arsenal should also recognize that science fiction and fantasy libraries and archives are really a triumvirate. One party consists of the creators: the authors, the filmmakers, the artists, the editors, etc. The second includes the scholars who have gone before us and have produced important research on SFF: at Cushing, we have works by and the archives of significant researchers such as Sam Moskowitz and Everett Bleiler.

And the final member of the triumvirate, just as important as the other two, belongs to the fans: the people who receive the stories, who find joy and meaning in those stories, whose hearts and minds are fired, touched, comforted, and excited by those stories. To that end, we also collect fanworks of all sorts: fanzines, fanfic, vids, and filksong (music generated by and tied to SFF fandom). No one can really understand the full breadth of the SFF world without understanding how readers and viewers interpret, discuss, and revise the creative works that they love.

Cushing Library is one of a small but expanding number of arsenals (or perhaps a more appropriate metaphor might be 'arks', as vessels designed to preserve) devoted to ensuring that the long, fascinating, rich, and complex chronicle of science fiction and fantasy is secured, safeguarded, and made accessible to present and future generations. There will always be an audience for stories of both what might be and what can never be, and there will always be people interested in the history and development of these stories. For those people, collections like ours exist.

4 / *BOUNDARY CROSSING, LIMINALITY, AND THE HUNGARIAN LITERARY FANTASTIC*

AN INTERVIEW WITH BOGI TAKÁCS, AUTHOR OF ALGORITHMIC SHAPESHIFTING & EDITOR OF THE TRANSCENDENT SERIES

by T.D. Walker

To be in a liminal state for long is a massive demand on one's energy. And yet this is something that happens to marginalized people all too often. I think a lot of my poems are about this kind of discomfort. And also, when a high-energy state is maintained for long, the release can be explosive.

\- BOGI TAKÁCS

Speculative poetry is a constantly-shifting market with a vast and diverse group of readers & writers. Today in our Q&A series, T.D. Walker (a talented poet in her own right and author of *Small Waiting Objects* from *CW Books*, 2019) touched base with one of spec poetry's most powerful voices, Bogi Takács. Editor of the Transcendent series for Best Transgender Speculative Fiction, winner of the *Strange Horizons* 2014 Readers' Poll for eir hypertext poem "You Are Here / Was: Blue Line to Memorial Park," Takács is also a reviewer, journalist, and holds Masters degrees in Psychology and Theoretical Linguistics, as well as attending the University of Iowa for a Ph.D. in Speech & Hearing Science.

Interstellar Flight Press: One of the striking elements of *Algorithmic Shapeshifting* (*Aqueduct Press,* 2019) is the way worldbuilding puts your reader both in this world and in other worlds, at times simultaneously, and others oscillating between them.

As a writer who works in both speculative prose and poetry, do you find that your approach to worldbuilding changes between each genre? Do the worlds presented in your poems push back on the forms you create with the poetic structures in ways they might not in prose? And how does the language of your poems tie in to that creation of these worlds?

Bogi Takács: I think that my approach to worldbuilding is roughly the same for both when I write prose and poetry. I generally start with visual imagery. Translating it into words is a separate process, and a very conscious and deliberate one. I do think that my poetry has a closer relationship to words, and—so to say—the surface form, than my prose does.

IFP: An overarching theme to the book is the idea of boundaries, those created and those transgressed. How did you want the poems to challenge your readers' ideas about boundaries, both personal and interpersonal? And since poetry collections guide their readers through arguments about the worlds they are set in and composed in, how did you view boundaries between the poems as you were assembling the collection?

BT: This is a really fascinating question, and now that I consider this topic of boundaries and crossing them, I feel it also applies to my prose. One of my own stories closest to my heart is "This Shall Serve As a Demarcation" (*Glittership,* Episode 3, 2015) which is very explicitly about demarcations and boundary-settings, both in the physical and the conceptual sense. This is also going to be the starting story in my upcoming debut prose collection *The Trans Space Octopus Congregation* (*Lethe Press*, 2019); the one that sets the tone for what will follow.

But this theme definitely appears in my poetry too. Boundary-crossing happened to me in a very physical sense because I'm a migrant. I also find myself thinking a lot about the boundaries of the body, probably related to my being autistic and not having a good sense of my body in space, but also possibly related to transness/intersex-ness. I had a lot of experiences, especially in a medical context, where people would not respect the boundaries of my body or even me as a person. I ended up changing my Twitter username to @bogiperson at one point because I wanted to see it all the time in my face that yes, I get to be a person too. I had trouble believing it. Now some people assume Person is my last name!

I'm not sure exactly how I want to challenge people's ideas of boundaries. I do think some boundaries are necessary and important, for example, the boundaries of my body are there for a good reason, and so are everyone else's. But other boundaries can be restrictive and even harmful; binary sex/gender policing, for instance.

I think one possible way of thinking about it is that from a certain vantage point, sets with sharply defined boundaries are just a special case of sets with less sharply defined boundaries. Generally, in high school math, one is only taught about the former, but the latter can absolutely exist . . . as much as mathematical constructs can be said to exist. Sharp boundaries can be more of an oddity than not, it all depends on the framework we use. And what we use depends a lot on what we are taught.

One more thing that might be interesting to contemplate is that boundary-crossings are often held up as something exemplary and crucial. "Genre-bending!" "Liminal!" And so on . . .

maybe even fetishized or exoticized, in a way. But boundary-crossing is not necessarily a comfortable experience. My Spouseperson, R.B. Lemberg, likes to say that liminality in the original folkloristics sense is—while something very important—generally uncomfortable, temporary, and dangerous. One is not supposed to hold a liminal position for a prolonged amount of time. But a lot of us are in these kinds of positions for longer. I am currently a "resident alien" in the legal sense, what is that? Or, as a nonbinary and intersex person, I am quite stable in these identities, but in society, there is very little room for them currently. People do not necessarily want to allow me to settle into them.

To be in a liminal state for long is a massive demand on one's energy. And yet this is something that happens to marginalized people all too often. I think a lot of my poems are about this kind of discomfort. And also, when a high-energy state is maintained for long, the release can be explosive.

IFP: The poems that stayed with me most after my reading the collection formed the "Two-Tailed Triptych" series, which explores the activities of the Two-Tailed Dog Party, a political party that parodies Hungarian politics: "The Ideas of March," "Why I Intend to Vote for the Two-Tailed Dog," and "Ode to the Ganymedean Telepathic Slime Mold." As a reader, I see this group of poems as both political commentary and as a statement of what speculative poetry can do as a genre. In his essay for *Poetry Magazine*, "The Politics of Poetry" (July 1, 2008), David Orr states: "Most contemporary American political poems are written for contemporary American poets, which means that political poems generally have more relevance to the politics of the poetry world than to the politics of America."

While your poems address politics in Hungary, they're set in Kansas, and I'd imagine a good percentage of your readers are American. Do you find that bringing elements of science fiction and "tropes of the dystopian subgenre," is a useful way to draw a wider audience to political poetry? Can we, as speculative poets, use the mode of the contemporary lyric to make a more impactful political statement by bringing in science fictional contexts?

BT: A huge chunk of my readership is people in non-Western countries who read in English. It is only a recent phenomenon that more and more Americans read my work (I feel like 2016 was a turning point for some reason, even before the American elections). This is also why I try to make sure that as much of my writing is freely accessible as possible, and use my Patreon to kind of subsidize this, because for many of my readers, $1 per month costs a lot more than for people who live in the US.

People often ask me to describe my audience and/or whether I write only for my own marginalized group. These days I write fiction and poetry exclusively in English. (A story of mine, *Forestspirit, Forestspirit,* originally published in Clarkesworld in 2015, was translated to Hungarian for the first time last year by Csilla Kleinheincz). I am not even sure who would be "my group" given that I am a Hungarian Jewish neuroatypical trans intersex person (etc.) who is an immigrant to the US, and all those identities do not necessarily occur together. Most of my relatives can't read fiction or poetry in English. Ultimately, I write for people around the world who are marginalized in some way, or in multiple ways—even if their specific marginalizations are very different from mine.

To address the second part of the question, I use the vocabulary of the speculative and the fantastic because it comes naturally to me. Part of it is because I grew up enjoying speculative work, both from the Western and the Eastern Bloc. Part of it is that my life experiences often do not fit into non-speculative framings. So yes, using those framings makes it easier to get my point across.

From an Anglophone point of view, it might be harder to notice the connections, but I feel like my work can be related to a long tradition of the Hungarian literary fantastic that often comes from a place of ethnic marginalization, and that strongly engages with its political context. Works like *Átyin Jóskának nincs, aki megfizessen* by the Hungarian Romani writer Béla Osztojkán (1997), or Serbian Hungarian writer Nándor Gion's tetralogy *Latroknak is játszott,* many of the *One Minute Stories* of Hungarian Jewish writer István Örkény and also his absurdist plays . . . or more recently the prose of Ádám Bodor and György Dragomán, both ethnic Hungarians from Romania who immigrated to Hungary, have been influential for me as a reader. I feel these works, to an extent, come from a similar position as especially Latin American and African magical-realist literary traditions.

(A side note: I am not dropping all these names for "cred" purposes, but because I hope that at least some readers might seek them out; some of these authors do have works available in English or other languages, and György Dragomán's breathtaking and magical novel *Bone Fire* is coming in English in 2021 from Mariner Books.)

Back to my original train of thought—it was a big turning point for me when I finally had access to a library with a considerable English-language collection (in Vienna, Austria) and read Ngũgĩ wa Thiong'o's *Matigari* (*Africa World Press,* 1998) and was stunned by just how *familiar* it came across; and also his nonfiction *Decolonising the Mind* (*James Currey Ltd/Heinemann,* 1986), where he explicitly discussed how non-Western peoples often only have dialogue with each other through Western literary centers. That really hit home for me, and since then, I have been explicitly trying to focus on this kind of decentering, solidarity and literature-building, with my own small tools.

These are mostly prose examples, but fiction was simply more available for me in translation in that formative phase. Now in the U.S., I can walk to the public library or take the bus, and get practically all the recent English-language releases; after several years, I'm still getting used to this, and it's amazing.

One thing that might be worth discussing related to audiences is . . . who buys my political poetry. I have sold poems to most of the major speculative poetry venues at this point, but my political poems are generally self-published through my Patreon (often sponsored by specific backers; thank you!). I have had a small amount of them published in general literary venues, but I feel like the non-speculative literary world has a much more convoluted, opaque, and lengthy process to publication compared to speculative venues, whereas my political poems often reflect on very immediate events and I would like them to be read right away. Of course, in a collection, it is not really visible which works appeared where, unless one scrutinizes the copyright page.

IFP: Are there collections that touch on the same themes that you'd like to recommend to readers of *Interstellar Flight Magazine*? Or are there others you've read recently that deserve mention?

BT: On the body, disability, I really enjoyed *Bodymap* by Leah Lakshmi Piepzna-Samarasinha (*Mawenzi House Publishers*, 2015). When it comes to political poetry, one of my favorites is *even this page is white* by Vivek Shraya (*Arsenal Pulp Press*, 2016).

Marginalia to Stone Bird (*Aqueduct Press*, 2016) *by* R.B. Lemberg is probably the most similar overall because we are married to each other, and some of our poems very directly reflect on each other.

Nature Poem by Tommy Pico (*Tin House Books*, 2015) has very little in common with my collection, but I loved it so much, I just want to tell everyone about it.

I read a lot of Hungarian poetry, I am especially inspired by early twentieth-century Hungarian poets (in translation: *In Heaven's Iron-Blue Vault* by Attila József, translated by Frederick Turner and Zsuzsanna Ozsváth (*Blood Axe Books*, 2009); *Foamy Sky* by Miklós Radnóti, likewise) and also late twentieth-century and contemporary Hungarian Romani and Jewish poets. I waited so long for Károly Bari's latest collection *Csönd* (*Kalligram*, 2017) and it absolutely blew me away.

Bogi Takács is a Hungarian Jewish agender trans person (e/em/eir/emself or singular they pronouns) currently living in the U.S. with eir family and a congregation of books. Bogi writes, reviews, and edits speculative fiction, and has won the Lambda Award in 2018 for editing *Transcendent 2: The Year's Best Transgender Speculative Fiction* (also a Locus award finalist book).

You can find em at Bogi Reads the World dot com, and on Twitter @bogiperson, and Patreon as @bogiperson.

5 / INDIE GAMES AND ACCESSIBILITY: A PERSONAL ODYSSEY

FINDING COMFORT IN GAMING AS A WOMAN

by Archita Mittra

Navigating [the gaming] world as a girl, to find the kind of game that you like (and can afford) is difficult. That's where indie games and accessibility come in.

Gris (Nomada Studio and Devolver Digital, 2018) is an exquisitely-crafted platformer that plays like a poem. It's deceptively short, not really difficult, and gorgeously rendered. Also, it's easily playable by both casual and experienced gamers. As therapeutic as painting in an adult coloring book, it straddles the line between "interactive art" and "video games." I recommend this game to people who're curious about gaming. Still, to this day, it's one of the games in whose art I can easily lose myself no matter how many times I play it.

I've had doubts about using the "gamer" label for myself—but I've accepted I'm someone who just likes to play games, and perhaps also talk about them. If a bookworm is someone who enjoys reading books, regardless of how many books they've read, then a gamer, as per my logic, would be someone passionate about gaming, about interactive and non-linear storytelling, and not defined by whether or not they own the latest PlayStation or Nintendo Switch console, or even if they've played the games that industry stalwarts consider classics.

Games have fascinated me for a long time, but growing up, I didn't get to play as much as I'd have liked. There were many practical reasons: For one, I was a girl, and secondly, I was a girl growing up in an Indian family.

In fact, I didn't possess a computer until middle school. Before that, I completed any schoolwork requiring a computer at my local cyber café, which was often crowded with neighborhood boys playing video games by the hour. The games mainly involved shooting people or racing through surreal urban locales on a motorbike.

Much to the surprise of the boys, the latter interested me, and I lined up to play *Road Rash* (Electronic Arts, 1991) on a Windows 98 desktop. It was exhilarating to completely lose myself as I raced for the finish line, as though my life depended on it.

The boys didn't really object to me playing. Sometimes we even helped each other. But they regarded me as an aberration from the norm.

We were civil, but we weren't friends.

My parents didn't approve of me hanging out in a local café by myself —and playing games on a computer I had to pay for. They insisted I use computers for "school work." They also insisted too much screen time would damage my eyesight. Perhaps "games" were not worth it. As the years went on, I frequented the cyber cafe less and less.

But then, the children's library I visited every two weeks for my supply of fantasy and sci-fi novels acquired a computer. It was ancient—a grey and white Windows 95 relic that ran tremendously slow and had *Captain Claw* (Monolith Productions 1997), a side-scrolling platformer some remember fondly even now. Initially, I found the story of a feline pirate hunting for treasure, fighting bosses, and escaping traps difficult. Eventually, I got used to it and played for an hour or two at a stretch. My library routine involved quickly returning and choosing two new books and assuming the lone computer that was unoccupied, proceeding to play *Captain Claw* until my mother dragged me away.

When I insisted my parents buy me a Playstation, they regarded the device as some new-fangled monstrosity, and upon hearing the price, straight-up refused. A cheap desktop with minimum RAM, lacking a graphics card, and a carefully-rationed internet connection which limited the choice of games, had to suffice.

Instead, I focused on Pinball, chess, and those agonizingly slow Windows card games. Meanwhile, I watched the boys in my cohort graduate to first- and third-person shooters and massively multiplayer online role-playing games. At home, I installed some old favorites (*Road Rash* and *Captain Claw*), discovered the sheer brilliance of cheat codes, and engaged in short free-to-play Flash games as well as virtual worlds online. In one instance, I remember installing *CounterStrike* (Valve, 2000), constantly getting killed, and finally crashing my desktop for good. My parents never forgave me for it, and the boys grew even more distant when I told them that *CounterStrike* really wasn't my kind of thing.

And as anyone will tell you, middle school can be terribly long—and I found a new solace in otome games or dating sims and visual novels. They granted me an imaginary social life and provided a semblance of gaming. I began with *Alistair++* (Sakevisual, 2010), moved onto the breathtakingly poetic *True Remembrance* (Shiba Satomi, 2006), and played trial versions of paid games—my avatars nursed dying boyfriends back to health, went on date nights in haunted mansions that always went wrong, and had an assortment of pretty anime characters to choose a romance with. Years later, I played *Doki Doki Literature Club* (Team Salvato, 2017) and decided to never ever return to the dating sim genre.

During my last year of high school, I stumbled upon the world of indie games. While looking for Red Riding Hood retellings, I came across a gothic/horror game called *The Path* (Tale of Tales, 2009) along with *Gone Home* (The Fullbright Company, 2013), a walking simulator-cum-mystery. Both broke the notion of what video games could do. There were no high scores to beat, monsters to slay, or cities to race through. Instead, what I had in my hands was interactive art.

Finally, in college, I had the good fortune of meeting a friend who let me check out games on his snazzy laptop. I played a few rounds of *Tekken* (Namco, 1995) with him which I didn't like, tried my hand at *Dark Souls* (FromSoftware, 2009) which was a disaster, and explored a magical cave in the thoroughly enjoyable *Rime* (Tequila Works, 2017). He even let me borrow games from his hard drive that would run on my slow and crippled laptop.

Of course, the games we like tend to say a lot about ourselves and our tastes. The magic realism of *Kentucky Route Zero* (Cardboard Computer, 2013) enraptured me, the finale of *Life Is Strange* (Dontnod Entertainment and Square Enix, 2015) devastated me and *What Remains of Edith Finch* (Giant Sparrow and Annapurna Interactive, 2017) left me speechless. I enjoyed the sibling bonding in *Brothers: A Tale of Two Sons* (Starbreeze Studios and 505 Games, 2013). *80 Days* (Inkle, 2014) brought back my nostalgia for text adventures, and playing the cyberpunk *Red Strings Club* (Deconstructeam and Devolver Digital, 2018) and the slightly supernatural *Oxenfree* (Night School Studio, 2016) made me realize my fondness for dialogue and choice-heavy narrative-focused games. Walking simulators seemed to me the easiest to get into, like *The Stanley Parable* (Davey Wreden, 2013), *Firewatch* (Campo Santo and Panic, 2016), and *Dear Esther* (The Chinese Room, 2012) while *To The Moon* (Freebird Games, 2011) recalled my love for visual novels. Owing to the constraints of time, I thought role-playing games wouldn't be up my alley, but I was pleasantly surprised by *Transistor* (Supergiant Games, 2014) and *Child of Light* (Ubisoft, 2014).

While I was in the middle of playing *Night in the Woods* (Infinite Fall, 2014), another friend expressed an interest in playing it with me, saying his computer was too old for the game to run. Playing together was an alternative kind of multiplayer experience. We argued over which dialogue option to choose or which part of the city to explore and all the time talked about the characters whose trajectories we decided. He also installed an emulator on my smartphone, thereby fulfilling my long-cherished wish to play *Pokemon Emerald* (Game Freak, The Pokémon Company, and Nintendo, 2004), which I'd seen engross my best friend in middle school.

Indie games made me realize that while not many of us may be able to afford the tech or even the games for that matter, there is a game for everyone if you look hard enough. And being a part of an inclusive gaming community that welcomes everyone regardless of their experience and gender is important—both for fostering a love for the genre and for making games accessible to all. At least from what I've seen, playing video games regularly as entertainment is a privilege.

But even those of us without access find ways to enjoy this privilege. We share Steam libraries, we go over to a friend's place to play a pre-installed game, we anxiously follow flash and discount sales on gaming sites to get a game or two for free. Or we pool enough money to buy them. Not all of us come from families or communities that encourage gaming. Navigating that world as a girl, to find the kind of game that you like (and can afford) is difficult. That's where indie games and accessibility come in.

Incidentally, *Gris* is a game about a girl who is unable to sing and who journeys from a colorless world to newer places of magic, life, and vitality. The game ends with her having found herself at last, away from despair and ready to sing, in a world of restored color and light.

But it took me years to find that game (and myself).

And I suppose that's a really beautiful metaphor for so many girl gamers out there.

6 / *DIVERSE SPACE OPERA, FIGHT SCENES, AND NANOWRIMO*

AN INTERVIEW WITH VALERIE VALDES, AUTHOR OF CHILLING EFFECT

by E.D. Walker

What can I say, I'm a sucker for power couples.

- VALERIE VALDES

Valerie Valdes is the author of *Chilling Effect* (*Harper Voyager*, 2019), first in a new series of fun space opera novels starring a Cuban-descended spaceship captain, Eva Innocente, and her misfit crew as they blunder their way through the galaxy trying to save her kidnapped sister from an intergalactic crime syndicate. Valdes is a member of the NaNoWriMo community and also writes short fiction and poetry, with stories in *Nightmare Magazine* and poetry in *Uncanny Magazine*. *Chilling Effect* is her debut novel and perfect for fans of the weird world-building in *Farscape* and the crew camaraderie of *Firefly*.

INTERSTELLAR FLIGHT PRESS: *Chilling Effect* is really fast-paced, and I thought the action scenes were particularly original and well done. Do you have any kind of martial arts background yourself? Did you do any special research to make the fight scenes more visceral?

VALERIE VALDES: My "special research" for fight scenes varied depending on what I was doing. I studied martial arts and stage combat a long time ago—shout-out to Chessmasters, 'sup my Rennies—and I relied on that primarily for sensory details. Stage combat especially is very focused on selling reactions, which I think is one of the most important parts of writing a fight; it's one thing to lovingly describe a punch being thrown, but if you don't then describe how the punch lands, it loses impact—pun absolutely intended.

I'm also a fan of kung fu, gun fu, and wuxia films, which tend to have the best fight choreography in the history of ever. They're not only amazing on a technical level, they also nail the emotional trajectory and stakes for the primary characters involved, and they're tonally appropriate to the situation. A fight scene in a comedy will be wacky and wild and fun, where a scene in a drama will be tense and brutal; compare, say, something from *Police Story* to *Sha Po Lang*, or *Kung Fu Hustle* to *Ip Man*. Seriously, go do it, everyone needs to watch more of these movies and then come fangirl about them with me.

IFP: A large component of this book is Eva's bond with her crew. How did you "assemble" her crew as you were writing? Was it a conscious process, "Oh, I need an engineer, a doctor, some muscle . . ." or did the characters emerge as you were writing? And, this might be mean, but do you have a favorite member of the crew? (Mine's probably Vakar.)

VV: Putting the crew together was a lot of fun. Mostly I thought about a combination of characters I loved from books, movies, video games, and TV shows, as well as my friends and family, and then mashed it all together. Considering logically what job roles would need to be filled on a small cargo ship was also part of the process; what kinds of skills could each person bring to the party, and how could they be showcased in the story? I also wanted there to be a good mix of backgrounds, ages and so on, and a variety of outside interests that not only gave readers a sense of each character, but also the wider universe of the novel and each person's place in it.

Once I started writing, some of the characters changed a bit from how I originally intended as their voices solidified in my mind—Min, for example, was initially much more formal and withdrawn, but after watching a few Korean soap operas I decided to make her more of a bubbly teenager. I also had a character who was part of the crew in the first draft, but who was way too badass and basically did all the cool stuff, leaving Eva sidelined in her own novel. I didn't kill that particular darling, but I did change his role entirely and give Eva all his awesomesauce moves instead. If I had to pick a favorite, it's probably Pink, because she's incredibly easy and fun for me to write; she's world-weary and snarky, but extremely caring, and I more or less just picture a hybrid of two of my friends and Laverne Cox and she writes herself.

IFP: I'll try not to spoil too much, but the romance in this is a bit unorthodox, as Eva's love interest is not human. What made you want to give your main character Eva such a different love interest than the norm? Did writing an outside-the-box romance present any challenges for you?

VV: Two words: *Mass Effect*. It's definitely not the first or only series to tackle romance between a human and a member of a different species, but it got me thinking about the concept more deeply and made me want to try my hand at it. What points of overlap might one find in courtship rituals, on a personal and cultural basis? What physical aspects could inform attraction on both sides, or make relations more complicated? What kinds of miscommunications might occur? How is a baby formed? And of course, on the Monster F***er Kinsey Scale, where would this fall? There's a big difference between, say, Aeryn Sun and Garrus Vakarian in terms of generally accepted concepts of attractiveness. Certainly, there had to be enough similarity between my characters for any connection to occur at all; that goes for any human relationship as well, but when you factor in an entirely separate evolutionary trajectory and its accompanying diversity of societies, things can get much more complicated if you let them.

I also didn't want this to function as a metaphor for any existing variety of marginalized human relationships, which is one path similar situations can take; the danger there is in dehumanizing or exoticizing those pairings and groupings and unintentionally implying that they're intrinsically alien in nature. Eva is pansexual, not because she's interested in someone from another species, but because she's attracted to people of all genders, as many people are.

IFP: Your bio mentions that you're an active member of the NaNoWriMo community (National Novel Writing Month). How did you get into NaNoWriMo? Do you feel like the NaNo experience and/or community is an important part of your writing process?

VV: I got into NaNoWriMo right at the tail end of college. I can't remember how I heard about it, but it seemed like an incredible challenge to write 50,000 words in a single month. I'd pretty much stopped writing fiction entirely at that point, and had been focusing on poetry instead—I had written a book of poems for my senior thesis, a few of which eventually found homes in various publications. But I was also participating in a fairly brutal online poetry workshop that ultimately did more harm than good, I think, and my productivity and confidence were both battle-damaged. The NaNo community was, by contrast, intensely supportive and focused on quantity over quality, which was incredibly freeing once I managed to get out of my own head enough to embrace the ethos. I failed the first two years I tried it, including my first year as a Municipal Liaison for the Miami region, but then I got the hang of it and started routinely churning out new novels every year. Most of them were unfinished because 50,000 words is apparently not enough for my brand of story, but every time I "won" it was proof that I could do the thing, and I leveled up a lot by doing so much so quickly.

Chilling Effect started as a short story, but I used NaNoWriMo to expand it into a novel, writing the first half in November 2014 and then finishing the rest over the course of the next nine months. I have three other novels I'm working on now, including the sequel and two completely separate fantasy novels, and NaNo helped me make huge progress with all of them. I also have NaNo to thank for helping me connect with local writers; I've been running a "shut up and write" group for several years now, and we're a pretty tight-knit bunch.

IFP: Book Two is called *Prime Deceptions* and is expected in 2020. For fans of *Chilling Effect* (like me!), can you give us any news about what's coming next? Will the romance continue?

VV: Trying to avoid spoilers . . . The crew's adventures continue as an unlikely ally gives them a big job that turns out to be very personal for one of the characters, very problematic for another, and downright traumatic for Eva herself as it digs into dark places from her past. New planets to explore, new people to meet, new secrets to reveal, and more of the same wacky action from the first book. And yes, more romance! What can I say, I'm a sucker for power couples.

Chilling Effect is available from Harper Voyager. Valerie Valdes attended the University of Miami, where she majored in English literature with minors in creative writing and motion pictures. She is a graduate of Viable Paradise and has taught classes in speculative short fiction writing. She also has over fifteen years of experience in copyediting for individual and corporate clients. Valerie has served as the Municipal Liaison for the Miami region of National Novel Writing Month for over a decade. She currently lives in Miami with her husband and children. Learn more about her on her website, candleinsunshine.com.

7 / *PHANTOM FARES*

A HAUNTING LYRICAL ESSAY

by Piper Daniels

Japan, 2011. A magnitude nine undersea megathrust earthquake hits Tōhoku with such force it causes the earth's axis to shift by several inches. Along the coastline, fifty fires ignite at once. An oil refinery explodes into flame and a thick black smoke billows from that burning. Moments later, a 133-foot tsunami rushes over the land, swallowing buildings and fishing vessels with terrifying, inevitable speed. Bridges and roads are annihilated, and at the Daiichi Nuclear Power Plant three reactors experience level seven meltdowns. From video recordings, a man can be heard screaming, "We've lost everything. Here is like hell on earth."

The lucky few who aren't swallowed up that day climb to the highest points of their roofs waving white flags in a desperate attempt to be rescued. From an aerial view, the flags look like ghosts floating up from doomed bodies, spirits tethered to the flesh in a rush to evacuate.

As children raised in the evangelical faith, the Book of Revelation, which prophesies the end of the world, was little more than a bedtime story to my sister and me. To lie on our backs in the tall grass and look at the sky was an act of meditation meant to prepare us for the End Of Times, when Jesus would return and bring the whole galaxy crashing down.

In spring, we watched the migratory birds head north for nesting, praying for their safe return along the flyway, between the breeding and wintering grounds.

We read these birds have a neural connection between the eye and the part of the forebrain known as "Cluster N," which becomes active during migration, enabling birds to literally *see* the magnetic field of the earth.

We wanted to go where they could go, see what they could see. We wanted our bodies to be built like their bodies, all mental maps, compass points, instinct, and light.

J. touched down into our lives one spring like a squall, then stayed on: a foul-smelling fog, a thick marine layer that would not lift.

J. was a hero in town because a cop who was chasing him shot him in the back of the head with a taser and somehow, he ripped it out, hopped a fence, and kept running, managing, that time, to escape.

We were not raised that way, to love boys like him, but she was tangled in him anyway.

Forest for the trees.

At a very young age, long distance migrant birds go their separate ways, forming strong attachments to potential breeding and wintering sights. Once the attachment is made it is rarely broken —the birds visit the same wintering sites every year.

In the aftermath of natural disasters like the one in Tōhoku, reports of supernatural experiences increase exponentially.

Five years after the earthquake and tsunami in Tohoku, Yuka Kudo, a sociology major, began writing her senior thesis on potential supernatural experiences that had taken place in the wake of the disaster. Kudo interviewed one hundred taxi drivers in Ishinomaki, the area that had been hit hardest. Many drivers refused interview, but seven of them reported remarkably similar stories—that of Phantom Fares. In each instance, a fare entered the cab, requested to be taken to a decimated location, and before reaching their final destination, vanished into thin air.

"No ghost was ever seen by two sets of eyes," wrote Thomas Carlyle.

The most frequently cited of Yuko Kudo's studies involves a cab driver in his fifties and the woman who got into his cab near Ishinomaki Station. The woman asked to be taken to the Minamihama district.

"The area is almost empty," the driver said. "Is it okay?"

"Have I died?" the woman replied in a shaking voice.

Perplexed, the driver looked over his shoulder and found that the woman was gone.

Tōhoku police are now collaborating with exorcists in the area.

She says it was good between them in the beginning. I tell her Heaven is ephemeral. That since Eve and Adam, Paradise has proved unsustainable. That even for far-ranging migratory birds who've made it to the tropics, paradise lasts but a single season.

When the world breaks apart the way it did in Tōhoku, ghosts rise up to fill the void.

In addition to the Phantom Fares, firefighters are repeatedly asked to respond to calls from a street that's been washed away by the tidal wave. Mothers report that the toys of their dead children are moving on their own.

Following the Antofagasta Landslide in Chile, sobbing and screaming has been ringing through the darkness for decades. A four-year-old boy dressed in white walks through walls and peers in people's windows.

Again in Chile, following the 2010 earthquake, shadows and disembodied screams rise from the bowels of the devastated parts of the city. Shadows can be seen crossing the Cardinal Raúl Silva Henríquez Bridge. Cell phones light up with incoming calls from disembodied voices that never quite connect.

After the 2004 Indian Ocean earthquake and tsunami, locals reported the spirits of wealthy foreigners stranded, lost.

106 years following the 1910 Avalanche in Wellington, WA,

reports of a ghostly woman humming and singing, reports of children playing, and screams so eerie they could only rise from the throats of the dead. "A century later," one woman reports, "they're still trying to find their way home."

I went once to the trailer park where my Sister and J. lived together. The furniture was expensive but littered with liquor bottles and overflowing ashtrays. I saw four-dozen holes in the wall she'd covered with posters. She was uncharacteristically quiet, and he stuck to her like a sun-warmed lozenge to a sweater. His pitbull ate my leather boot in a single bite.

The night following the visit, I dreamt of the *Odyssey*, of Odysseus sailing beyond the dawn to the untouched, sunless edges of the earth. I watched the ghosts in the meadow of Asphodel flit like shadows.

I woke with traces of the river Lethe on my tongue, remembering that to drink there was to be stripped of one's identity.

Sometimes a boy is not a boy at all. He is only a way to disappear.

Despite what sophisticated navigators they are built to be, there are times when migrating birds lose their way. They fly past their destination in the spring overshoot, ending up too far north. Or in the case of reverse migration, a young bird's genetic programming fails, and they end up as stranded vagrants thousands of miles out of range. Or in drift migration, when birds are simply blown off course. Or in abmigration, wherein birds from one region join those from another and end up migrating back, immersed in their new population.

In many cultures, birds are seen as harbingers of death. They steal souls from the dying, embody spirits of the dead, or act as psychopomps, shepherding souls of the departed from this world to whatever comes next.

Sparrows, for instance, are built slight and hollow of bone so they may carry home lost spirits of the dead.

Sisters are similarly made so that whomever is lost may live on in the other one lightly.

Many experts have tried their hand at explaining supernatural phenomenon that follows disaster.

Theology Professor Hugo Zepeda claims that the psychological damage suffered by survivors of a single tragedy is so similar that they achieve a "collective projection, which means that they feel or see more or less the same things."

"The perceiver [of ghosts] is prepared for the experience on the basis of his or her having, so to speak, been eaten by pests. The condition is one of eroded defenses, of vulnerability," Elizabeth Robinson writes.

Some people believe ghosts roam the earth because of unfinished business.

Others believe they remain because we are unable to let them go.

I am hoping this boy is a broken mirror I can bury by moonlight.

I am hoping my sister knows that the story of migration is a story imbued with the hope of returning, and because of that, I will lie in the tall grass between the wintering and breeding grounds, and I will watch for her.

8 / *RIVERDALE, WRITER'S BLOCK, AND NAVAL WARFARE*

AN INTERVIEW WITH R.F. KUANG, AUTHOR OF THE DRAGON REPUBLIC

by Holly Lyn Walrath

> *There is no "perfect mood" for writing–when you're on deadline, you just have to get the work done, whether you feel like it or not.*
>
> \- R.F. KUANG

If you're into SFF books, you've probably heard of R.F. Kuang's debut bestseller *The Poppy War* (*Harper Voyager* 2018). It was a Goodreads Choice Award finalist (twice over), Nebula Award finalist, Locus Award finalist, and winner of the Stabby, Crawford, and Compton Crook Awards. Kameron Hurley calls its sequel, *The Dragon Republic* (*Harper Voyager,* 2019), "A blistering, powerful epic of war and revenge that will captivate you to the bitter end." We can attest: This series packs a major punch of history, badassery, and grit.

INTERSTELLAR FLIGHT PRESS: We love the book covers for *The Dragon Republic* & *The Poppy War*. Can you tell us anything about the behind-the-scenes decisions that lead to such a badass cover series?

R.F. KUANG: I actually participated very little in the cover art! All the credit goes to JungShan, the artist, and the wonderful design team at Harper Voyager. The whole process was very smooth. My editor asked me if I had any ideas or preferences, and I said I thought perhaps a blue and silver color scheme would make sense–which, turns out, was what they already had in mind. JungShan created another illustration of Rin that I just absolutely fell in love with. We pretty much went with the first thing we came up with; we all liked it so much. I think covers for sequels tend to be easier, because you already have an aesthetic set up by the first, and you just need a variation on those themes.

IFP: A little birdy told us that you love *Riverdale.* Are there any other shows or films you're really into right now? Are there any shows that have influenced your writing?

RK: *Riverdale* is SO MUCH FUN. The perfect mixture of weird, bizarre, and campy. And everyone is so attractive. I love that Archie basically exists to take his shirt off and make poor decisions. Hirum Lodge is Daddy.

Film/TV doesn't influence my writing much. I stick mostly to twenty-minute comedies that I can work into my lunch break or watch while working out. Right now, I'm obsessed with *Brooklyn 99* and *The Good Place.* Anything Michael Schur has worked on, really. I don't have enough hours in the day to spend on longer dramas anymore, though I really wish I did.

IFP: You're currently pursuing an MPhil in Modern Chinese Studies at Cambridge University, which seems like a lot of work to juggle between being a bestselling author! How do you make time for writing, and what drives you to come back to the page?

RK: It's very hard, and I'm not sure I have a good time management system down. Term time was tough. Either I fell behind on book stuff, or I fell behind on school stuff. I chose to fall further behind on book stuff because at the end of the day, I prioritize academics. The term is over now, so I've had some more flexibility to work on Book Three. I think I've gotten pretty good at working through writer's block because I've realized there is no "perfect mood" for writing–when you're on deadline, you just have to get the work done, whether you feel like it or not. I have a bunch of little productivity tricks—using a Pomodoro timer, setting daily word counts or revision page counts, listening to music—that in tandem provide sufficient motivation to bang some words out. If all else fails, reading a few hundred pages of good writing usually does the trick. Watching other people work magic with words always jumpstarts my brain to try to attempt the same.

IFP: So much of your love of history comes across in your books. When did you first become interested in history and why?

RK: I'm not sure it's possible to answer that question. It's like asking someone, "when did you first become interested in stories." Likely, at some point in my distant past when I first became sentient?

IFP: *The Washington Post* calls *The Dragon Republic,* "A study in every kind of violence . . . Kuang pulls from East Asian history, including the brutality of the Second Sino-Japanese War, to weave a wholly unique experience." Your books delve into the complicated, bloody, and often contested events in history. Tell us what intrigues you about these historical events and how you approach translating them to the page for a modern audience.

RK: I study modern Chinese history and literature, so it's natural that it inspires most of my fiction. I take a very syncretic approach to my academic and literary work; almost all of the cool/freaky/weird things I come across in my course reading gets spun into an episode in my books.

The question of how I translate them for a modern audience is interesting. See, I am the modern audience—I'm situated in the present day, so I can't help but understand historical events through my 2019 worldview. In a sense, I don't have to do translation at all, because I'm just presenting historical events to readers in the way that I, someone born in 1996, understand them. So I don't consciously worry too much about whether historical events will make sense to readers; if they make sense to me, then it's fine. On the other hand, I do have to think about whether someone not in my field will understand certain literary allusions, terms of art, signifiers, symbols, gestures, etc. (This isn't just a modern/historical issue, it's a Chinese/Chinese-American/American issue.) So I do often spell out the context behind a lot of images that wouldn't need that same explanation if the novel were written in Chinese for a Chinese audience.

IFP: What is your favorite thing in *The Dragon Republic*?

RK: I like the naval battles! Dragons in Chinese mythology are often closely associated with water, so it makes sense that most of the action in Book Two happens over rivers or at sea. I got to play around with river warfare tactics, secret pirate cities, and all makes and models of different ships. (I got very into this—I have a whole research document titled "ship porn.) There are quite a few episodes in Chinese history that deal with naval warfare—most famously the Battle of Red Cliffs—so I enjoyed spinning my own version of those. I didn't have any previous academic experience in naval warfare, so I did a lot of research in tactics and equipment, which was tremendously fun.

R.F. Kuang is the Nebula, Locus, and Campbell Award nominated author of *The Poppy War* and its forthcoming sequel *The Dragon Republic*. She is currently pursuing an MPhil in Modern Chinese Studies at Cambridge University on a Marshall Scholarship, where her dissertation examines propaganda literature by Northeast writers during the Second Sino-Japanese War. Check out her website rfkuang.com, to stay up to date with her writing.

9 / *CATS IN SCIENCE FICTION FILMS*

A SHORT HISS-TORY OF THE KEY ROLES PLAYED BY FELINES

by John Tuttle

When we think of pets or domestic animals in the sci-fi genre of cinema and television, we might automatically call to mind the iconic sled dogs from *The Thing* (1982) or the little English-speaking alien disguised as a dog in the original *Men in Black* (1997). However, another fond and furry animal appears in science fiction even more so than its canine contemporaries: the humble cat.

With their graceful maneuverability and attractiveness, cats have found their way into science fiction plots throughout film history, whether as the random "guinea pig" for a mad scientist's latest experiment or a reluctant stowaway who fights Kree soldiers in space. Some cats have become iconic emblems of science fiction, while most have become utterly crucial to the plots they partake in. And some simply serve to mystify us.

In early sci-fi, cats often keep scientists company in their isolated laboratories. One instance of this is the random pussycat in *This Island Earth* (1955), In the film, three scientists discuss the sketchy circumstances of their work for a mysterious man named Exeter and their apparent captivity. A cat announces its presence with a screeching meow, giving the scientists quite a start. After feeding the hungry kitty, the scientists conclude Exeter could be listening to them (indeed, he is) and change the topic of their discussion. Ultimately, the cat causes the change in conversation which limits Exeter's knowledge of the Earthlings' plans of escape.

Another early sci-fi flick featuring felines and scientific machinery is *The Fly* (1958). The story features two fine felines, M'sieur Tom and Dandelo. Unfortunately, Dandelo happens to be in the wrong place at the wrong time. Namely, when scientist Andre Delambre needs a biological test subject for his next teleportation experiment. Though teleportation doesn't go down too well for Dandelo, the cat serves as a necessary link in a chain of tests. After a few adjustments, Andre intends to move on to human "guinea pigs." But another unforeseen mistake mars his test and creates a human-fly hybrid, one of the most nightmarish sci-fi scenarios seen on screen.

By the 1960s, cats or cat-inspired characters make frequent appearances in action-packed TV programs. Additionally, many of the feline characters are often portrayed as feminine. Cat Woman from the Adam West *Batman* series is one example. Zaybo from the 1960's show *Lost in Space* is another. In the episode "The Haunted Lighthouse," an alien boy has an invisible companion he calls Zaybo. While invisible, Zaybo can create an audible meow and fits nicely in the boy's two cupped hands. However, when visible, the cat is a ferocious lion. Then again, Zaybo also appears as a seductive woman, an example which fits that sixties stereotype mentioned earlier.

A few months after "The Haunted Lighthouse" aired, *Star Trek*'s "Assignment: Earth" hit TV audiences with another female shape-shifting cat. In the episode, secret agent Gary Seven has a feline for his closest companion. Her name is Isis and, as we see near the episode's end, she seems to be more than your everyday pussycat. While resting on a couch, some see her as a woman while others still see her as a cat.

Star Trek's feline fixation can be seen in later continuations and spin-offs. Eg: Data's pet cat Spot in *Next Generation* or M'Ress in *Star Trek: The Animated Series*. M'Ress is actually an example of the Caitian race, which, as you might guess, is a race of cat-like humanoids. If you wish to be entertained by feline re-envisionments of the show's main characters, check out Jenny Parks' illustrated book *Star Trek Cats* (2017).

Chronologically, *Star Trek* carries us into the nineties, where we find *Men in Black* (1997), a splendid mash-up of sci-fi and comedy. In this film, an Arquilian (alien) scientist named Gentle Rosenburg owns a cat named Orion. Though a ferocious, bestial insectoid kills Rosenburg, Orion is left untouched. Only by the climax of the movie do we begin to realize the marble on Orion's collar is something much more than a décor piece. Within the little translucent orb snuggly rests a micro-galaxy: a unique and full cosmos all of its own. Orion has been its unassuming guardian.

Most recently, a lovable "cat" appears on the big screen next to one of this year's most significant superheroes: Carol Danvers, a.k.a. Captain Marvel. The cat named Goose shadows Danvers and Nick Fury in *Captain Marvel* (2019), one of the latest installments within the Marvel Cinematic Universe. Goose is revealed (spoilers!) to be a Flerken, a cat-like creature whose mouth possesses Kraken-like tentacles outstripping Goose's relative size.

Although Captain Marvel is the film's most important character, one can make an argument that Goose runs a close second. In one scene, Goose protects the good guys by literally devouring their enemies while a shocked and two-eyed Nick Fury looks on.

In another scene, we see Fury lose an eye when Goose slashes his face.

But, Goose's most critical role is his consumption of the coveted Tesseract, an artifact containing an infinity stone. As a Flerken, Goose's internal anatomy includes a pocket dimension which explains how he was able to swallow and keep down the Tesseract. In an after-credits sequence, we see Goose barf up the Tesseract. For decades, Goose kept the Tesseract safe, serving as a temporary, biological lockbox for an object of immense power and destructive potential. It was Goose's quick thinking (or random craving) that allows for the Tesseract to fall back into the hands of the somewhat competent agents of S.H.I.E.L.D., making possible the whole chain of *cat*-astrophic events that is to ensue.

As we have explored in detail, cats have inspired many sci-fi creatures. Cats themselves frequent on-screen stories of flesh-eating blobs, secret agents, glowing celestial stones. Even more frequently, they have provided fundamentally critical aspects to the storylines of science fiction on TV and the big screen alike.

10 / *UNABASHEDLY HOPEFUL, HEARTBROKEN, AND SILLY*

AN INTERVIEW WITH CHRISTIAN MCKAY HEIDICKER, AUTHOR OF SCARY STORIES FOR YOUNG FOXES

by J.T. Morse

> *Kids have a lot of walls in their heads just aching to be knocked down.*
>
> *- CHRISTIAN MCKAY HEIDICKER*

Who has a demon-hunting cat, writes spec fiction for young readers, and purposefully became addicted to video games to fuel his writing? Author Christian McKay Heidicker. After spending several years working in education, developing instructional comic books for a non-profit, and teaching creative writing at Broadview University, Christian McKay Heidicker shifted his focus to writing. We're glad he did. His latest book is *Scary Stories for Young Foxes* (Henry *Holt and Co.*, July 30, 2019). Interstellar Flight Press contributing writer J. T. Morse had the opportunity to exchange words with this cat-loving storyteller and avid fan of Jordan Peele.

INTERSTELLAR FLIGHT PRESS: Let's kick off with

a chat about video game addiction. Is there really such a thing, Christian? Give us the scoop on how video games have informed and influenced your writing, in particular, for your first book, *Cure for the Common Universe.*

CHRISTIAN MCKAY HEIDICKER: I played a LOT of video games in high school. A lot.

A friend and I failed all of our AP exams because we were too busy trying to defeat Final Fantasy VIII (a terrible game that no one should play). After that, we had to take a good look at ourselves and wonder what we were getting out of our time in front of a screen. I stopped playing completely when I decided I wanted to become an author.

It was only after I was given the idea of video game rehab, by a friend, that I picked the controller back up for research efforts. After that, I purposefully got myself addicted to games by playing them for eighteen hours a day for a solid month. Then I took a month off from technology and caffeine and sugar and anything addictive. It was in that purified state that I wrote *Cure for the Common Universe.*

IFP: For your upcoming release, *Scary Stories for Young Foxes*, you collaborated with an illustrator. Tell us about why you chose to work with Junyi Wu and share some of the ups and downs of teaming up with a visual artist.

CMH: I chose Junyi because:

A. Her work is amazing.

B. I'd never seen anything like it before. It's a little fairy tale and a little naturalistic with just a dash of horror.

Initially, we were tempted to go with someone like Jon Klassen (he illustrated *Pax* by Sara Pennypacker), but we were trying to create something unique. A recognizable style didn't feel right. By the time Junyi started working on the art, I was pretty much finished with the book. So, there wasn't a lot of back and forth.

Publishers usually organize that kind of stuff, and I'm lucky that my editor, Christian Trimmer, even asked for my feedback in the first place. Once we chose Junyi, things were easy for me. I just sat back and watched the beautiful art rolling in. I even bought some of the originals and plan to hang them in my office.

IFP: Rumor has it that you're a huge Bram Stoker, H.P. Lovecraft, and Edgar Allen Poe fan. What do you find inspiring and admirable about these horror-writing icons and their work?

CMH: Haha. I'm not a huge fan of any of those guys! That was just a marketing hook my publisher came up with.

However, I do enjoy the first hundred pages of Dracula, a couple of Poe poems, and a handful of Lovecraft's more atmospheric tales. But those last two authors are hugely problematic. It's hard enjoying Poe's dark side when you know he married his thirteen-year-old cousin and abused her. And Lovecraft is the incel to end all incels.

Fortunately, some savvy creators like Matt Ruff and Jordan Peele are finding ways to pay homage to Cthulhu while calling out the authors' misogyny and racism. To me, that's pretty exciting. I would've tried something similar, but, y'know, it's a kids' book about foxes, so I just made my Lovecraft story about alligators.

IFP: Give us some insight into why writing speculative fiction for Middle Grade and young readers appeals to you so much.

CMH: I could sit here for four years and try to concoct the most original idea in the universe, and I guarantee someone in the adult world has already done it. Not so in kids' books.

Video game rehab? A girl trapped in a 1950's horror movie? Classical monster stories retold with baby fox kits? Boom. Brand new. But not so marketable to adults. Kids have a lot of walls in their heads just aching to be knocked down. Also, you can be unabashedly hopeful, heartbroken, and silly with kids. And that's me. I care very deeply about these foxes. Even if it doesn't seem like it with some of the horrible things that happen to them.

IFP: We couldn't let this interview close without inquiring about your demon-hunting cat. Every writer should have a supernatural feline by their side. Tell us more, please.

CMH: Lucifer Birchaus Morningstar (a.k.a. Lucy) is the light of my life—my fiancé knows and accepts this.

I was walking through Best Friends Animal Adoption— just to look (aren't you always there to just look?)—when I walked past what I thought was an empty kennel. A tiny black paw reached out and snagged my shirt. I turned and found golden-green eyes staring back at me and instantly fell in love. My ex-girlfriend was with me and said she didn't want to get a cat. You can probably guess how that relationship ended.

Lucy and I share dreams sometimes. I once dreamed that I was running, and she was running beside me. I woke up to find her legs scampering on the bed, her eyes still squeezed shut. Another time, I had a nightmare that there was a skeletal woman hiding behind the drapes in my living room, skin dripping off her bones. I woke up when Lucy sprinted into the bedroom, licked my cheek, and demanded to be cuddled. She's not a licker. Ever. But I could tell she was terrified. I think she saw that skeleton woman.

Christian McKay Heidicker reads, writes, and drinks tea. Between his demon-hunting cat and his fiddling, red-headed girlfriend, he feels completely protected from evil spirits. Christian is the author of *Scary Stories for Young Foxes*, *Cure for the*

Common Universe, and *Attack of the 50 Foot Wallflower*. He lives in Salt Lake City, Utah. Learn more about him at cmheidicker.com.

11 / *STRANGE BODIES*

PROJECT RUNWAY, FINDING MY QUEERNESS, AND BODY MODIFICATION

by Presley Thomas

> *. . . Coming out is itself its own kind of body modification as it changes the way others see you. Often with horns on your head instead of your shoulders.*

Project Runway began on December 1, 2004, on a small, ambiguously gay cable channel called Bravo. The show helped build the channel's audience and, often for the first time, brought gay culture into peoples' homes. Even those unfamiliar with gay culture found the talent of PR's budding fashion designers a draw. Viewers wanted to see something created from start to finish, from a piece of fabric to wearable design.

I started watching Project Runway in 2012 with my mother. After we both came home from work, I'd sit on the couch while she never slowed down, always ironing clothes even when the show was on. Her arms moved with the iron across the wrinkled fabric, her eyes focused on the television as designers competed in challenges. As we watched, we made comments on the garments as if we were fashion executive judges ourselves. We had no experience, but we had each other, and I hoped that would be enough. That a single truth of the many things she loved and acknowledged about me wouldn't change everything. That I wouldn't get voted off the family and be asked to pack my things and go.

A year and a half out of college, I was still living at my parents' home and working an hourly job in healthcare. It wasn't so long ago that my parents married off my straight twin with all the love and affirmation he and his wife could handle. I wasn't yet brave enough to tell them the truth out of fear for what that might mean for my health and safety.

Mom and I made our own family while my dad worked in California. He was an occasional houseguest. I often made an effort to go into Mom's room when I came home after going out. I was dating men for the first time in earnest, but I could only tell her what parts of my day I knew she could handle.

Even though my parents sometimes complained about me living at home, Mom and I were each other's anchor. My family had roots in the Southern Baptist Church, so I didn't imagine my queerness would be received well. On top of still depending on my parents and feeling stunted in building my own family, even as my siblings had begun to form their own in college and married women soon after, I was living in limbo.

Now, in 2019, Project Runway has moved back to Bravo with a facelift for Season 17. It features Project Runway winner Christian Siriano from Season 4 as the designer's fashion mentor and another tall, blonde model, Karlie Kloss, as host. Episode 2 opens with the designers coming into their workspace with exhibitions from Simon Huck's brand "A, Human." featuring body modifications and flesh-colored protrusions on various parts of the body, each one with a design team of three to form a collection that showcases each strange difference:

1. Glow Necklace, soft yellow lights embedded behind a flesh tone around the neck, famous for being worn by Kim Kardashian.
2. Neck Ruffles, large ruffles that protrude like fleshy gills around the neck.
3. Chest feathers, designed in partnership with Chrissy Teigen, flesh-colored angels wings in miniature across the top of the chest where cleavage might be.
4. Shoulder horns, just like they sound, dark devil-like horns pointing inward towards their model's freakishly symmetrical faces.
5. Back Scaffolds, mirrored ridges centered on the lowered back protruding like many small spines.

As with previous seasons, many of the male designers are gay in addition to the mentor Christian Siriano. We learn that Kovid and his boyfriend of many years had to leave their small village in India to make sure they were safe from persecution. In response to stress around his sexuality and presentation as a more feminine gay man, he engages in meditation in his native language each morning before they leave for the workroom. A nod to spirituality often left blank for queer individuals.

Since it's still early in the season, others are still unknown, but as they move into their co-living space, sexuality is revealed as they chose roommates. Different genders show different levels of comfort with other genders.

In the finished runway show, back scaffolding gives way to backless dresses. Shoulder horns create an opportunity for bare shoulders. The glowing necklace moves the eye up to the neck of long, lean models. The designers in team neck ruffle use it as an opportunity to flare out their fashions below. Team chest feathers leave the top half of their styles open, though often poorly segmented down the middle, hiding the modification more than needed.

Team neck ruffles stood out the most to the judges for their high-quality, cohesive work. Sebastian Grey pulled out a win with his sheer dress with ripples of off-white fabric that flow down his model as she walks down the runway. He is another gay designer this season, from Colombia, who wants to use his ambition to create a fashion brand that reaches beyond his native country's borders.

Team Neck Feathers falls short this round. When pressed, they say their work is for yet another wealthy white woman. Kovid makes his plea to the judges about his love of women as a more feminine gay man and wanting to celebrate them through fashion. His work acts as more of a cover for the body modification than an accent. He is one of two left at the end to stay or go. His other teammate, Frankie, who was on the bottom in the previous episode, gets told it's her time to go instead.

As I watched the most recent season of Project Runway, I realized that coming out is itself its own kind of body modification, as it changes the way others see you. Often with horns on your head instead of your shoulders.

There isn't a uniform for being gay. There isn't a brand or line of clothing. I didn't have the ability to modify my body to show my inward self.

As I started dating men, I began to feel what my siblings told me about their romantic relationships over the years. I never experienced the feeling of attraction until my 20's when it became harder and harder to hide. I felt happier, lighter; I was letting go of shame from an evangelical upbringing. I knew I was different. It was harder and harder to hide.

When Mom and I were watching season 10 of Project Runway I saw these gay men working and crying and succeeding in a reality show. I watched her celebrate and enjoy the products of their labor. It made me feel like maybe, just maybe, she would one day accept me, too.

One night, I came home from a date with the man who would become my first boyfriend. I was floating as I walked to my mother's door, light creeping beneath it as I stood in the dark hallway and knocked. Her voice, muffled through the door, told me to come in.

I lay across her king size bed and buried my face in her soft comforter. She wore a terrycloth robe and a white facemask with a white towel wrapped around her head after a long hot bath.

"How was your night?" she asked.

"It was great. I went on a date."

"How was she?"

"He was great. I like him a lot," I said, smiling into the folds of the bedspread.

"He?" she asked. I could hear the tears forming in her voice as she reached down beside her nightstand.

She pulled out a copy of a celebrity gossip magazine I recognized. My dad bought them at airports for her when he came home from California, a sign of love. She flipped manically through the pages to find the wedding announcements as she choked a question through her tears, "Is this what you want?"

"Sort of," I said, "but those are lesbians," she was pointing to two smiling happy women with her manicured nail: Ellen DeGeneres and Portia De Rossi.

I'd like to say that my mother accepted me as easily as she accepted the designers on Project Runway. From then on, I was treated as a broken thing to be fixed. If I had wings, they were bat-like and leathery, and whether I had horns depended on how I chose to behave. My choice to come out meant I had to choose between my family and the Southern Baptist values I grew up with, values that actively erased me—or embrace my sexuality like my straight parents and siblings had done to create a life that supported mutual flourishing as we moved through life together. It would look different, but it would be ours: foggy, amorphous, and unknown. I had to quit pretending my family and their vision of faith fit my world. That my body knew something my heart didn't.

That day I told my Mom the truth, I didn't have a garment to show her I was gay. I didn't have the ability to modify my body to show my inward self. There isn't a uniform for being gay. There isn't a brand or line of clothing. I didn't even mean to tell her. It just felt so good to be alive as a gay man than it ever did to hide it.

12 / *SPINNING TALES, CHINESE EMBROIDERY, AND MUSICAL COMPOSITION*

AN INTERVIEW WITH ELIZABETH LIM, AUTHOR OF SPIN THE DAWN

by E.D. Walker

> *I would write stories to accompany my short compositions when I was a kid, and that helped me stretch my imagination and gain confidence as a writer.*
>
> - ELIZABETH LIM

Elizabeth Lim is the author of *Spin the Dawn*, a sweeping YA fantasy about a young girl named Maia who poses as a boy to compete for the role of imperial tailor at court. She ends up on an impossible journey to sew three magic dresses, from the sun, the moon, and the stars. Part Mulan, part Project Runway, this immersive first installment of *The Blood of Stars* series released July 9, 2019 from Random House. In addition to writing novels, Lim worked as a film and video game composer and holds a doctorate in music composition from The Juilliard School.

INTERSTELLAR FLIGHT PRESS: Did you do any research for the tailoring and fashion portion of this book? (Just how much Project Runway did you have to watch?) Do you know how to sew yourself? Where did you get your inspiration for all the incredible court dresses and outfits that you describe in the book?

ELIZABETH LIM: I actually didn't watch any Project Runway while writing *Spin the Dawn* (shh lol). I've seen plenty of seasons though, so I didn't need any help jogging my memory. A lot of my research came from my childhood memories: my grandmother was a seamstress, and my mother loves embroidery and all sorts of needlecraft, so I grew up around lots of sewing in the house. While I was writing *Spin the Dawn,* I also borrowed all the books from the library on Chinese embroidery and traditional dress and relied on my childhood hobby of fashion drawing to create the court outfits described in my book. The setting of my book isn't Ancient China per se, but the fashion does draw heavily from historical dress (and was inspired by my visit to the Metropolitan Museum's amazing exhibit "China: Through the Looking Glass" in 2015).

IFP: I saw on your website that you're a composer and a fan of movie scores. (I am also a huge movie score geek.) Do you have a favorite movie composer or film score? Do you ever compose music to go along with your novels? Does composing music use the same parts of your brain that writing does, or are different muscles in play?

EL: I love this question! I don't have a favorite movie composer or film score—I have too many to list! But the way I started out writing fiction was through music: I wanted to become a film composer, so I would write stories to accompany my short compositions when I was a kid, and that helped me stretch my imagination and gain confidence as a writer. And yes, I'm a firm believer that composing music uses the same parts of my brain as writing: I always try to pay attention to the harmony of my words as well as their rhythm, and the structure of my stories often relate to musical forms I learned in school.

IFP: You mention on your website that you're a new mom. Has that been challenging for you? Any tips for all the other working writer moms out there on "making it work," to quote Project Runway?

EL: I am still figuring this out! I'm not sure if I have any tips on how to "make it work," but I've learned to be easier on myself and to allow myself to rest. When my baby was first born, I pushed myself to write whenever she was sleeping, and I got tired out very fast. Now I sleep when she sleeps, and I snatch whatever writing time I can in the mornings and evenings. It's not the most ideal schedule, but I'm still working consistently, even if a bit slower!

IFP: Book Two in *The Blood of Stars* series has been announced already. For fans of *Spin the Dawn* can you give us any news about what's coming next?

EL: Without giving anything away, you can expect a darker tale with plenty of new challenges for Maia. And there will be more Lady Sarnai!

To learn more about Elizabeth Lim, for links to her work, and ways to purchase her books, check out her website, elizabethlim.com.

13 / *PERCEPTION, UNCERTAINTY, AND DREAD: THE HORROR OF PERSPECTIVE*

HOW DO YOU MAKE A NOVEL FRIGHTENING?

by Caitlin Starling

Horror movies have a hundred tools to create tension and fear in the audience: sound cues, lighting, the speed of shots, the suddenness of reveals. Visual and auditory content is powerful, immediate, and lends itself well to layering. Movies hold attention well and are short enough to be consumed in a single sitting.

By contrast, books have less to go on: we can only somewhat control the pace at which our audience consumes the story through tricks of tension, chapter length, complexity or simplicity of prose. A novel is longer than a movie, and slower too, each detail taking more time to communicate. The chances of a reader devouring the whole book in one go are slim, and even in a best-case scenario, the early moments are divorced from the finale by many hours, softening the impact of parallelism and callbacks. And while length can be its own tool (would *House of Leaves* have been as effective as a snappy novella, instead of having long meandering footnotes that are suffused with atmosphere and throw confusion over the specifics of the plot?), it can also drag and delay and bore.

Authors use prosody and character voice to create atmosphere, and little tricks of language to signal *things are about to get bad.* We can also borrow from the successful tactics of movies, with variable success. A jump-scare can be mimicked *somewhat* by the abruptness of a transition, but it's just as likely to be confusing as frightening.

Where books can shine in a way wholly their own, though, is in *perspective.* Just as a long tracking shot can summon up dread, the coldness or closeness of the narration can affect our perception of the actions going on in the story. And a book's potential for intimacy in its narration can be turned and twisted to surprising effect.

In *The Luminous Dead*, my first novel, we follow a young woman named Gyre down into a treacherous cave. She goes down alone, with only a high-tech suit and a voice in her ear to help her survive. The suit introduces as many problems as it does solutions. It keeps her safe from dangerous falls and manages any medications she might need, but it also requires surgical installation. It renders her environment via sonar in an attempt to keep her concealed from unknown threats, but in doing so introduces room for computer error or lost information.

It leaves her completely at the mercy of her handler, Em, who can control Gyre's body and influence—or completely change—what Gyre sees.

Gyre experiences the cave at a level of remove that by its very nature introduces errors, misunderstandings, and omissions. The effect is quietly compounded as we, the audience, experience the cave by way of Gyre's biases, weaknesses, assumptions, and fears. Here, the use of third-person narration plays a clever trick. If the book was written in first person, we would almost expect it to play with the unreliability of the narrator. But we're trained to think of third person as being factual, accurate, a representation of the world as it is, with just the distance of the camera from the characters up for question.

So when, in *The Luminous Dead*, Gyre finds incontrovertible signs that somebody else is in the cave with her, that her sensors also see, we default to believing that those signs are real. But when in the next moment that sign is proven to be impossible, and Gyre has no explanation for it and offers no explanation for it to the reader, it throws into question the very reality and reliability of what we're reading. Was that bolt even there? Was there somebody else on that rope? Can we trust that Gyre would even notice one way or the other?

And that's the root of the horror of *The Luminous Dead*. There's an omnipresent sense of dread throughout, heightened by the fact that even as Gyre can't trust but *must* trust Em, we can't trust Gyre but must in order to continue reading. Even as Gyre can't see without the limitations of her headlamp, her sonar reconstruction, and the dubious help of Em's computers, we can't see without Gyre. We can't see free of her paranoia, her anxiety, her delusions.

We can't see what lurks around the corner, but we feel like we *should* be able to, that in another book, we *would* be able to at least see the hint of what is coming.

Instead, we're trapped in the suit with Gyre, with no way out, and no relief.

No breaks.

There's only Gyre, and the cave, and the constant dread and drudgery.

14 / *SPACE OPERA IS HAVING A MOMENT AND WE LOVE IT*

MELODRAMA, SPACE WARFARE, AND ROMANCE, OH MY!

by E.D. Walker

I want to talk about space opera. Like many of you, I imprinted on *Star Wars* at a young age, and now any story emphasizing space warfare, melodramatic adventure, interplanetary battles, chivalric romance, and risk-taking must be consumed. Immediately.

If the SFF books coming out over the next few months are any indication, space opera is having a moment and I'm beyond excited. Considering the new *Star Wars* trilogy, the popularity of *The Expanse* TV show and, in the book world, the monumental success of Ann Leckie's *Imperial Radch* series of space opera novels, this makes sense. If you've imprinted on *Star Wars* like me, you're going to have a happy next few months until you remember you're still stuck on Earth.

Here are some upcoming new works that I can't wait to read:

Got a hankering for "melodramatic adventure?" Pick up *Pure Chocolate* (*Angry Robot*, 2018). It's the second book in Amber Royer's *Chocoverse Series*; the cover describes the story as "space opera meets soap opera," and the author calls the book a "telenovela." Chocolate is Earth's last great export and everyone else in the galaxy is killing to get their hands on it. The heroine is a culinary arts student caught stealing chocolate who has to go on the run.

Perhaps you need some chivalric romance? Try *Polaris Rising* by Jessie Mihalik (*Harper Voyager*, 2019). A space princess flees an arranged marriage and teams up with an outlaw. During their adventures through intergalactic space, they fall for each other. Does this couple sound a little bit Han and Leia-esque? Uh-huh. It's one of my favorite ships, and I can't wait to read this book.

What about characters taking risks *in space*? Try *Chilling Effect* from Valerie Valdes, (*Harper Voyager*, 2019.) According to the author, her heroine makes risky decisions but all in service to save her sister! This book also has adorable space cats. How can you resist the adorable space cats? I don't think I can.

Last but not least, how would you like some good, old-fashioned SPACE WARFARE? (I don't know why but it just seemed wrong not to put that in caps. It feels like a phrase that should be accompanied by trumpets and fanfare, no?) Here's where I go off on a slight tangent: Where is the line between space opera and military science fiction? Is there one? *Should* there be one? I personally read both, and for me, it's more of a sliding scale than an either/or situation. I guess if the book is strictly about military personnel with no other space opera trappings (like a galactic empire) then it doesn't belong under the space opera umbrella. Usually, though, for some books, the needle swings more toward space opera, some more toward military science fiction. Okay, tangent over.

Anyway, if you'd like some fun and snarky SPACE WARFARE with a side of queer romance you could try *The Widening Gyre* by Michael R. Johnston (*Flame Tree Press,* 2019). (I need to add a small disclaimer here that Michael is a close friend of mine, but this book has been getting great reviews and buzz so I feel good including it.)

Other Space Warfare books that I'm excited for are the "space caper" *Finder* (*DAW*, 2019), from Hugo award winner Suzanne Palmer, and the bonkers-looking *Gideon the Ninth* (*Tor*, 2019) by Tamsyn Muir which smashes fantasy (think swords and necromancy) with sci fi (think spaceships and intergalactic politics). And the cover is FANTASTIC, and yes, I do judge a book by its cover. Sorry. Not sorry.

Last but not least, the second novel in Gareth L. Powell's Embers of War series, *Fleet of Knives* (*Titan Books*, 2019), features a former warship helping a mysterious generation ship in deep trouble with some dangerous aliens.

15 / *GOTH WEIRDNESS, SLAVIC FOLKLORE, AND OHIO*

AN INTERVIEW WITH EMILY A. DUNCAN, AUTHOR OF WICKED SAINTS

by J.T. Morse

I like making things and then breaking things.

- EMILY A. DUNCAN

What do the state of Ohio, lovers of Slavic folklore, and the Sandra Dijkstra Literary Agency have in common? Spec fiction author Emily A. Duncan. Born and raised in Ohio, Emily works as a youth services librarian when she's not putting pen to paper to fashion thrilling YA fantasy novels. Her latest book is *Wicked Saints* (*Wednesday Books,* 2019). Interstellar Flight Press contributing writer J.T. Morse had the splendid opportunity to grill this quirky Kent grad/lover of Dungeons & Dragons about all things Emily A. Duncan.

INTERSTELLAR FLIGHT PRESS: From your public bio, one could glean your educational background and your love of video games and Dungeons & Dragons. But we're curious to hear about the deeper elements of what makes Emily A. Duncan tick and why you write the type of stories you do.

EMILY A. DUNCAN: I like making things and then breaking things.

When I was a kid, my brother and I would both get LEGO sets for Christmas, and then I would build all of them because he would lose interest. Writing a book—building a world—isn't that much different for me. I like the act of construction and deciding what might mirror our actual world and what might . . . not. The core of what I write, I think, and what is most interesting to me, is investigating the lines between humanity and monstrosity (and sometimes divinity) and how those lines might intersect. Sometimes that's the act of construction, but more likely, it's the act of destruction, just like knocking apart all those LEGOs.

IFP: Seeing as *Wicked Saints* is somewhat of a dark fairy tale, were you a fan of fairy tales when you were a child, or did the love of folklore come about, for you, as an adult?

EAD: I always took a particularly keen interest in the villains in fairy tales.

My mom always likes to tell me that I wanted to play the role of the big bad wolf in any productions of 'the three little pigs'; which, who wouldn't? But I definitely took a more dedicated interest in them when I was in college and grad school. It was then that I really started delving into Slavic folklore.

IFP: Did you know that *Wicked Saints* was going to be a part of a trilogy when you started, or did the concept for the Something Dark and Holy trilogy come along after you had finished writing book one?

EAD: I thought it was going to be a duology!

Book one was going to follow Nadya and book two would follow Serefin and, while that still is the case, it was my agent who suggested it become a trilogy. Having written the second book, there is literally no way I could have wrapped up everything in two books! And I'm a big fan of the structure of trilogies, so I'm happy with how it worked out.

IFP: Tell us a bit about your experience publishing with *Wednesday Books*, including whose idea it was to use deckled edging for the pages.

EAD: Working with *Wednesday Books* has been *amazing!*

I feel deeply lucky to be able to work with them. It's a very good feeling to have a book that is, frankly, *weird* and have everyone on your team just get it so completely. I think it was my editor's assistant who suggested the deckled edges because it would make the book look more like a blood mage's spell book!

IFP: Let's talk cover design. Covers are so vital to the book-selling industry these days; they are the face of the story. The cover for *Wicked Saints* bears some interesting details. Without giving any spoilers, can you explain how some of the elements and images on the cover relate to the story?

EAD: It's very goth and very metal, much like the book.

It took a long time to get to the cover that's on the shelf now and I *adore* it! It doesn't actually show a particular element that is in the book—Maybe the monastery? But that's only in the book for a chapter—but rather, it invokes the atmosphere of the book really nicely. I love how intricate and oppressive the building is, and that it, kind of, looks like it could be the cover of some random *Gormenghast* edition.

IFP: Can you give our gothic-fantasy hungry readers any news about the status of the next two books in the *Something Dark and Holy* trilogy and maybe speculate as to when they might be hitting shelves?

EAD: If everything goes as planned . . .

I'm finishing up book two now and it'll be out sometime in early 2020! I call it my cosmic horror forest road trip book. It is deeply weird, and I love it a lot. Book three is in the very early stages, I'm still hammering out how it's going to all finish up, but it will follow along in early 2021.

IFP: Heading home, where would you say is the creepiest or most YA horror-story inspiring place to visit in Ohio? And, while we're on the subject, are there any writing festivals or literary conventions in Ohio that readers and/or writers should know about?

EAD: Oh, Ohio is *super haunted.*

I grew up in southern Ohio, and while I never visited the local haunted house site in my hometown, I grew up in the kind of woods where you didn't really have to go very far back into them to stop hearing any kinds of sounds of civilization. But the Hocking Hills were nearby, and there were all kinds of creepy places in Old Man's Cave. There's a place called the Devil's Bathtub, and it is both beautiful and slightly terrifying. When you drive into Clear Creek Park, there's a giant rock hanging over the road known as the Witch's Rock. The whole state is haunted. And Ohioana and Books by the Banks are two very good book festivals in Ohio!

IFP: Lastly, we would love to get three six-word sentences from you: one about *Wicked Saints*, one about your experience of being a writer, and one about something bizarre or obscure about Emily A. Duncan. Thanks for indulging us.

EAD:

Wicked Saints: Gothic weirdness drenched entirely in blood.

Writing: Both exhilarating and tedious at once.

Me: I like to keep my secrets.

There you have it, readers, straight from the goth-writer's mouth

—all that you need to know about Emily A. Duncan and her latest release *Wicked Saints*, book one of her *Something Dark and Holy* YA fantasy trilogy. For links to her work and ways to purchase her books, check her out on glitzandshadows.tumblr.com.

16 / NO ROOM IN NARNIA

REVISITING CHILDHOOD CLASSICS AS AN ATHEIST

by Erin Becker

My particular inability to lose myself in these worlds as an adult is tied to my no longer believing.

Revisiting beloved childhood novels can be a fraught process. So it was with some ambivalence that, as part of the research for my MFA at Vermont College of Fine Arts, I picked up my old copies of C.S. Lewis' *The Lion, the Witch, and the Wardrobe* (1950) and Madeleine L'Engle's *A Wrinkle In Time* (1962).

My edition of *Lion* has a color map on the inside back cover, one I'd been obsessed with as a child. It features a drawing of Aslan, his mane set off in crimson light against an epic night sky. And I'd reread my copy of *Wrinkle* so often as a kid that the spine is held together by masking tape now turning stiff at the edges. When I sat down with them, I was ready to go back through the wardrobe and greet Mr. Tumnus again. I was ready for Aunt Beast to wrap me in her warm furry arms.

I was also aware that both Lewis' and L'Engle's stories were deeply informed by Christian theology. As a kid, this influence was a plus. I was the girl who went to church every week, wrote poems to Jesus in my journal, and taught Sunday School as soon as I was old enough.

But by my mid-twenties, I was an atheist. There was no scene at the dinner table, no stomping out of the church after a bigoted sermon. Just a slow unwinding of faith until I didn't believe any of it anymore. Leaving the church was so anticlimactic that sometimes I forget how important being Christian was to me, until it wasn't. But I got a reminder of just how fundamental this shift has been when I tried to go back through the wardrobe into Narnia, to tesseract with Meg one last time.

When I was young and religious, these writers took me on adventures that not only felt deeply imaginative but also deeply real. Aslan gave his life to save Narnia, and this "magic from before the dawn of time" mirrored the power of Jesus' resurrection. When, in *Wrinkle*, Meg and Charles Wallace spot the evil Black Thing while visiting the planet Uriel, they watch Uriel's inhabitants fighting the malevolent force by dancing and singing a loose translation of a few verses from the Old Testament. The lyrics reminded me of a song I sang in church. I could finally be a part of the mythic battle.

But what once felt like an opening up to the weird and the wonderful around me now feels like a closing down. The Christian worldview that seemed so mysterious and all-encompassing when it was the only one I knew now seems like a limited narrative decision. In *Lion*, the New Testament allegory is so literal, the assumptions so *assumed*—that the Emperor is good because he is the Emperor, that humans should have power because they are human—that rereading it felt like I was trapped in a wardrobe myself. A wardrobe that would open not to a magical world, not to some unknowable core of things, but simply to another wardrobe, and another, on and on into a tautological infinity.

L'Engle's work leaves a little more room for ambiguity than Lewis' does, like when Mrs. Whatsit gives Meg "her faults" as a gift, foreshadowing how they'll "come in handy" when she travels to the planet Camazotz. Yet these moments of gray shade into black and white when Meg must face evil directly. Mrs. Who tells her, "The foolishness of God is wiser than men; and the weakness of God is stronger than men." What once read as subtlety now seems like a uniquely Christian brand of paradox, copied and pasted from every Sunday morning of my childhood. It felt like L'Engle had promised me the stars—then given me a Bible lesson on the hand of God in the night sky.

I don't think you have to be Christian to enjoy these books. I definitely don't think being Christian *means* you'll enjoy them, either. (*Wrinkle*, in particular, has been critiqued by fundamentalists for its secularism.) But I do think that my particular inability to lose myself in these worlds as an adult is tied to my no longer believing. Turning the books' yellowing pages feels a little like the last time I took communion. A glistening cup. The smell of old paper. The moment the wine-sip reaches the tongue. The way the words sound in the mind. The ritual is the same, sure. But the signifiers no longer hold any meaning.

17 / *KOREAN FOLKLORE, BIG SPACE EXPLOSIONS, AND MATHEMATICS*

AN INTERVIEW WITH YOON HA LEE, AUTHOR OF NINEFOX GAMBIT

by Michael Glazner

Folkloric creatures don't necessarily follow rules as though they came out of Dungeons & Dragons. Rather, the rules and constraints that Min has to confront are usually social and ethical more than rules of magic.

- *YOON HA LEE*

Yoon Ha Lee is not only a master of short fiction but is also known for complex folkloric space opera that redefines the genre. He is the winner of the 2016 Locus Award and a nominee for the Hugo, Nebula, World Fantasy, and Arthur C. Clarke Award. *The New York Times* called *Ninefox Gambit* (*Solaris,* 2016) "A tight-woven, complicated but not convoluted, breath-takingly original space opera." Following his *Machineries of Empire* trilogy, Yoon Ha Lee has released *Dragon Pearl*, a middle-grade space opera under Rick Riordan's imprint (*Disney Hyperion*, 2019). *Dragon Pearl* tells Min's story: a thirteen-year-old girl descended from fox spirits, who leaves her planet to find her brother.

INTERSTELLAR FLIGHT PRESS: What made entering into a partnership with Rick Riordan to publish Dragon Pearl attractive? Why was this the best way to tell Min's story?

YOON HA LEE: Two reasons: When my daughter, who was then a tween, learned I had an opportunity to write for Rick Riordan's imprint, I knew she would have killed me if I'd turned down the opportunity! She's a big fan of Rick's.

And the other reason is money. Middle-grade science fiction pays much better than adult science fiction, on average. My daughter is now fifteen and in ninth grade, which means we're soon going to be facing her college bills.

As for Min's story, that's actually the other way around. I didn't come up with Min and her world until I had to devise a proposal for Rick Riordan Presents. I was thrilled that Rick was promoting mythology-based fiction from many cultures, and I figured that no one else was going to be pitching Korean mythology space opera.

IFP: What makes a story qualify as space opera? What are five must-read/see space operas and why?

YHL: My criteria are very simple: big space explosions, bigger-than-life personalities, and lots of adventure, although there are lighter and darker varieties of space opera. My five would be:

1. Star Wars—pretty much the one you have to know if you're going to write in the genre.
2. Margaret Weis' *Star of the Guardians* series, which follows an exiled lady starfighter pilot, the king of a lost dynasty, an ambitious warlord, and more.
3. If you like the grimdark edition, I'm fond of the over-

the-top bloodfest that is Warhammer 40,000. I don't play the miniatures game because it's spendy and the thought of painting that many minis makes me want to hide, but it's a lot of fun.

4. Ann Leckie's *Imperial Radch* trilogy, wherein a ship's AI exiled from its own body seeks revenge for the death of its beloved captain, setting in train a series of events no one could have anticipated.
5. *Legend of the Galactic Heroes: Die Neue These* — an intensely political anime in which two starfaring powers and their respective military geniuses face off. If you like that, the novels by Yoshiki Tanaka on which it's based are mostly available in English translation, and if you're really hardcore, you can also look up the original anime (*Die Neue These* is a remake).

IFP: The *Machineries of Empire* trilogy hinges on mathematical rules and axioms. What rules and constraints will readers see Min struggle against in *Dragon Pearl*?

YHL: I played fast and loose with Korean folklore in *Dragon Pearl*, and in any case, folkloric creatures don't necessarily follow rules as though they came out of Dungeons & Dragons. Rather, the rules and constraints that Min has to confront are usually social and ethical more than rules of magic. She has the power to shape-shift and can use it for the first time, but as she learns, just because you have power doesn't mean you know the right time to apply it.

IFP: What universal archetypes will readers find in *Dragon Pearl*? Which archetypes showed up in *Dragon Pearl* that also made appearances in *Machineries of Empire*?

YHL: Both Min from *Dragon Pearl* and the undead general

Jedao from *Machineries* are tricksters; appropriately, both are associated with foxes. Min's friend Haneul is a loyal, studious friend who is always about following the rules—I'm pretty sure that personality type has existed since there were rules to follow. And her other friend Sujin is a troublemaker, although maybe not as much of one as Min herself. Beyond that, there's the dragon pearl itself, one more magical artifact in a parade of artifacts out of folklore and imagination.

IFP: What ideas or themes do you return to in your writing, and what has that told you about yourself?

YHL: Warfare, imperialism, culture clashes, math. A pretty good reflection of my nonfiction interests. My mother finds my fascination with military history completely baffling, but she still enables me when I ask for research help!

IFP: What ideas do you hope readers of *Dragon Pearl* walk away with?

YHL: Mostly, I hope readers have a fun time with the book. If any of them are inspired to write their own stories, of whatever kind, that would be excellent!

Yoon Ha Lee is the author of the middle-grade space opera *Dragon Pearl* and the *Machineries of Empire* trilogy. His short fiction has appeared in *Tor.com, Lightspeed Magazine, Clarkesworld Magazine, The Magazine of Fantasy and Science Fiction, Beneath Ceaseless Skies,* and other venues. He lives in Louisiana with his family and a very lazy cat—and has not yet been eaten by gators. Check out his website YoonHaLee.com to read his back catalog of short stories.

18 / *WHAT ELSE IS THERE TO SAY ABOUT THE JOKER?*

A DISCUSSION ABOUT WHETHER THE LATEST JOKER FILM IS A THOUGHT PIECE OR HARMFUL JUSTIFICATION OF OUR SOCIETY'S DARKEST PROBLEMS

by Archita Mittra and Kaylee Craig

Perhaps, if the film had chosen to engage more deeply with its subject, if it had chosen to be more intersectional and political, it would have been more relevant and a more fitting commentary of our times.

- ARCHITA MITTRA

Editor's Note: Given the amount of media coverage surrounding Joker (2019), I wanted to explore the film in a different way. When I put forth whether anyone wanted to review the film, two of our writers were interested. Kaylee Craig and Archita Mittra graciously agreed to collaborate on the following article, resulting in a back-and-forth conversation about the film, what it misses, and why it's worth discussing despite its harmful aspects. We here at IFP acknowledge that these harmful points deal with the lived experiences of many in our audience, and it is our goal to provide a space for conversation while respecting those experiences.

Major spoilers ahead, read at your own risk.

INTERSTELLAR FLIGHT PRESS: How does Joker play off of its predecessors such as the 2008 movie *The Dark Knight*? Given that Todd Phillips has confirmed how the film is supposed to be vague and open-ended, what did Joker add to the social discourse of the time we are living in as of now, one that is as highly polarized and characterized as the Trump era?

Kaylee Craig: *The Dark Knight* came out before the election of President Barack Obama. *The Dark Knight* took the mindset of America at the time, a society focused on the war on terror, gun violence, and a struggling economy, and heightened these fears cinematically, succinctly capturing the distress under the two-term presidency of George W. Bush. The hero of the film remained as the primary focus, but the relationship between him and the Joker could not be brushed off as simply a hero/villain dynamic like the two other films in this trilogy. Heath Ledger's Joker preyed on our sense of morality and confusion, through Batman gradually resorting to vigilantism from his previous position of moral authority.

Joker (2019), by comparison, plants us right into the chaos of our times through the eyes of the *villain* instead of the struggling hero. Played by Joaquin Phoenix, *Joker* now serves as an obvious social commentary piece. He is humanized, and the line between villain and the human underneath is now blurred. It's fitting for audiences in a time where our inner demons are given a social media presence and voice that inevitably creeps into our offline lives.

Our modern times are undeniably reflected in this parallel universe. We come to empathize with Joker as he struggles to live as a normal citizen from a struggling working-class background in a decaying metropolis. Fresh out of Arkham State Hospital for the mentally ill, he is forced into reality and a society that rejects him daily and violently. He wears two masks, as a clown in his day job and as a "happy", fatherless, caretaker, and "normal" citizen in his bleak daily life, he is the epitome of a social outcast and underdog that we pity.

Through his perspective and power as the narrator, we come to see how normalcy and complacency are stranger than their counterparts. He struggles to healthily cope with what is largely out of his control and a general feeling of dissatisfaction all around him through his stand-up comedy and obsession with wanting to become a famous comedian who has it all, much like the comedian he idolizes, Murray Franklin (played by Robert De Niro). Fed these cultural narratives of rags to riches and survival of the richest all his life and throughout the film through different successful and influential idols, he believes in his dream so much so that his mind starts to confuse fantasy and reality. When his fragmented reality is forced into the spotlight and questioned, he takes the last plunge into the madness that these cultural narratives manifest for the working class.

> *You never know if what he's saying is real . . . Whatever he's saying, it's very real to him. Whether it is objectively real, that's questionable. But for him, it felt real . . . It's really left up to you, to the audience, to decide what you think is real or isn't.*
>
> - *JOAQUIN PHOENIX, PRESS INTERVIEW*

It is easy to blame the current president for these problems, especially when he only fuels the fire with his own tools of oppression and denial (e.g. tweets and every press conference ever), but these problems have existed for years as we can see through the Bush presidency, and even before that. As has always been the case, film and television of the horror, psychological thriller, and tragic comedy variety have a subtle way of revealing the problematic cultural narratives of the given time period they respond to. *Joker* excels in this and doesn't shy away from utilizing our empathy to have us understand where we need to draw the line and what we need to change to save ourselves before our own inner demons consume us whole. And I would be remiss to not mention that these inner demons are entirely influenced by us being the product of our environment, and more specifically, our relationship to the state, an institution that is meant to provide and protect. How can a social institution do that in an individualistic society influenced by capitalism and cultural myths that are normalized daily? How can the state and its representatives separate themselves from the very environment that they share with their constituents? They can't, and we are seeing this for better or worse today in this age of technological innovation where we are given the tools to manifest realities we once only dreamed of.

For Joker, the pistol Arthur Fleck was given at the beginning of the film becomes his weapon for manifesting that reality, a piece of technology that destroys; only then does he become accepted and seen. So, this film asks us, how are we as a society with our cultural narratives and technology strengthening the power our nightmares and dreams have on each other? And in this Trump era, how do we recreate a sense of normalcy . . . that doesn't further oppress like it always has?

Archita Mittra: *Joker* does an okay-ish job at portraying class struggle and inequality within the capitalist framework. There's a pivotal scene near the end, where Arthur's depression, alienation, and frustration (stemming from his working-class background and a mental illness he has no resources to treat), is channeled into a moment of all-consuming rage and chaos ensues. It's a harsh reminder of just how cruel the system that we belong to can be, in which the creation of people like the Joker, is a mere by-product of its own toxicity. Yet, the film's politics are often intentionally and annoyingly vague. The Joker self-proclaims himself to be apolitical, yet he is lauded as a vigilante and the symbolic leader of the riots, by the countless working-class citizens dressed in clown-masks.

But the Joker is far from an "Everyman" figure, and neither can he adequately represent the struggles faced by the working class. At the end of the day, he is still a white cishet man, with clothes on his back, food in his larder, and an apartment to return home at night. Yes, it is heartbreaking when he is fired from his clown-job and when his Black therapist is forced to discontinue their sessions owing to a lack of funding, but he is still privileged among the lot of underprivileged whose stories are seldom told.

There are countless other people, belonging to minorities, and struggling with disabilities and battling sexism, racism, queerphobia and other evils each day, while trying to make ends meet. Of course, this point isn't to invalidate the Joker's suffering, but rather to point out how any depiction of class-struggle can never be so black and white. The unequal power dynamics in the "rich vs poor" divide, cannot exist without considering most importantly, issues of race and gender because otherwise, it becomes all too simplistic. The specificities of the diverse communities that make up a country like America dissolve in a sea of white-washed homogenous clown-masks.

Thomas Wayne who is easily an allegorical stand-in for Trump, only talks of the "less fortunate," even referring to all of them as clowns, but the "less fortunate" isn't one homogenous community, and neither does the film focus on building a sense of solidarity among different marginalized groups or adequately show how different communities are often pitted against and end up oppressing each other. Of course, having a one-man film that doubles up as Phoenix's resume for the Oscar application, doesn't leave much scope to engage with intersectionality. But perhaps, if the film had chosen to engage more deeply with its subject, if it had chosen to be more intersectional and political, it would have been more relevant and a more fitting commentary of our times. Yes, it provides Batman's arch-nemesis with a definitive origin story, but it doesn't delve too deep into the systemic and material conditions that supposedly create such people, and neither does it tell its audience how to be better. And by pitting Thomas Wayne as Arthur's personal villain, as well as the ultimate threat that must be eliminated at whatever the cost, also ignores the systemic causes that repeatedly reinstate such figures in positions of power.

IFP: What about the film's treatment of mental illness?

Kaylee Craig: The difference between Joker manifesting his dream of being a comedian and a person who does the same with their own dreams but with far more resources, support, and favored socio-economic status is that one outcome is seen as "crazy" and the other is seen as heroic. And I use "crazy" here as a comment on how someone like Arthur who has struggled with his mental health neurologically and emotionally, and comes from a poor and abusive background, is unjustly portrayed as "crazy" (a common theme in all media representations of "mentally ill" individuals that are automatically villainized based on socio-economic status). If we didn't shut out and isolate the individuals who need the most resources and support, then our society could be more united as a whole, but this isn't currently and hasn't been the case for America. Instead, we see a rise in people suffering from depression and anxiety across all social and economic classes, dwindling funding for social services and support unless it's a part of the psychiatric-pharmaceutical complex, and resorting to violence whether through cyber-bullying or mass shootings.

Archita: In the end, we are left with Lawrence Sher's

gritty cinematography and Phoenix's spectacular acting in a cinematic landscape of death, decay and social apathy, that despite trying to, doesn't mirror the horrors of the real world, as faced by countless real people. It isn't a revelation that a broken society is responsible for creating the likes of the Joker, nor that compassion and empathy are what we precisely need to counter it, and in that regard, the film has nothing new to add to the discourse, because it doesn't have anything new to say.

Kaylee: The way you brought in race and gender into this discussion as well is beyond significant. While I analyzed the film from the point of view of someone who struggles with mental illness herself and limited myself to seeing the film through that lens, I failed to take into account the other missing aspects of this film that only continue to silence communities that couldn't possibly relate to such a film.

While *Joker* gave us the space to recognize what was not being said or critiqued about our own society, because films and other cultural mediums are undeniably a product of their timing, the space given was too open in such a way that there are far too many questions for the audience without guidance towards answers. I think more than anything, what *Joker* did bring into the spotlight was the growing problem of gun violence and unrest that we can no longer ignore. The fact that military personnel and other law enforcement were warned about attending screenings of this film, and security was increased during opening week, shows that not only are incels still active (and represented in this film) but gun violence, in general, is an epidemic that is not being addressed as much as it should be. We are living in a time where there is a constant fear or terror that another shooting could occur anywhere at any time, and yet the current administration that is meant to uphold its duty of protecting citizens, is finding it too irrelevant to do so. This is nothing new, but this film just solidifies that in the most depressing way possible.

Archita: Yes, I absolutely agree. I think when Hollywood is investing so much money and effort to making a film like *Joker* that can easily be misconstrued as an incel film or one that tries to justify gun violence, especially with the anxiety over heightened security during screenings, it should have done so with more nuance and sensitivity. As you rightly said, the film ends with far too many questions without providing any guidance towards answers, which makes it almost flippant and irrelevant.

Of course, some might argue, that films, like any other art, doesn't owe its audience anything, but given our current political environment, I'm sure we'd all agree that we desperately need narratives that accurately reflect the world we live in and show how the citizens of Gotham and the audience, both inhabiting a broken system, can learn from our mistakes and do so much better.

And choosing to be apolitical is still a political stance that can only come from a position of privilege and entitlement. *Joker* deliberately plays it safe and director Todd Phillips has confirmed how the film is supposed to be vague and open-ended, so that the audience can derive whatever interpretation they prefer, from it. Such a stance automatically distorts or even nullifies any subversive potential of the film, particularly when Philips already feels that "woke culture" has ruined comedy.

NEW AND FORTHCOMING TITLES

FROM INTERSTELLAR FLIGHT PRESS

EXCERPT: THE MANTICORE'S VOW

THE AUTOMATON'S TREASURE

by Cassandra Rose Clarke

I sat on the deck of the Ocean's Rose with the only book I'd managed to shove in my trunk before I had to leave my homeland forever: an illustrated history of the Qilari swamps. It was an old book, a gift from some visiting dignitary or another who had heard about my love of the swamps. When I was a little girl, I'd been mad about them. I thought I'd outgrown the obsession, but banishment will send you wheeling back to your childhood, apparently.

I was sitting in one of the rickety wooden chairs left out for passengers, alone except for the handful of sailors scrambling in the ropes overhead. The book lay open in my lap, but I couldn't concentrate on the words. I'd read it twice on this trip already, and there were still another two months before we landed in Lisirra, the city that would serve as my prison.

A family came up on deck, shattering the peaceful, windy silence. They looked Empire, like most of the people on this ship, and they had a tottering little boy who ran up to the railing and peered over the edge, shouting about sharks. His mother joined him, saying something I couldn't make out over the wind. They were speaking the Empire tongue, which was my entire reason for eavesdropping. I'd certainly need to be fluent soon enough.

The wind picked up and turned the pages of my book, landing on a dog-eared illustration of the Qilari crocodile, mean-faced and spiky-tailed. I shut the book and settled back in my chair. The masts were silhouetted in the sun. Two sailors scurried along the tops of the sails, shouting to each other. Empire again, although a dialect I wasn't familiar with. I caught every three or four words—ship, sight, direction. Cannons.

Cannons? My Empire was rustier than I thought. The Ocean's Rose was a passenger ship, and decidedly not one for aristocrats or the wealthy. I doubted they had cannons on board.

The two sailors were joined by a third, a woman who swung in on a rope. She landed lightly on her feet, balancing herself against the top of the mast. I couldn't see her face, but she nodded her head vigorously and then swooped away again, dropping to the deck a few paces away from me and rushing off toward the captain's quarters.

The family was still standing by the railing. They'd been looking down at the sea, not up at the sky, and missed that bit of excitement.

And then an officer came on deck.

He walked over to the family first and spoke to them in a slow, hushed tone. I tilted my head toward them, trying to be inconspicuous, but I couldn't hear. The mother and father exchanged brief, worried glances; the son was still clinging to the railing. A pause. Then the mother wrapped her arm around her son's shoulders and led him away, speaking to him as she did so. I caught, "a bit of time down below—" before the officer appeared next to my chair, the chain draped around his shoulder glittering in the sun.

"Good afternoon, Lady Anaja-tu," he said.

"That's not my name, " I snapped, more harshly than I'd intended.

He faltered. I'd confused him. "Excuse me," he said. "My, ah, lady—"

I scowled, but I didn't correct him a second time.

"I'm afraid we'll be sailing into a storm soon. We're asking that all passengers retire belowdeck. I'll send a porter around when it's safe for you to come back up."

"A storm?" The sky was a blank curve of blue, like the side of a flawless Saelini glass vase. "Are there even any clouds out?"

"Yes," he said, his voice firm. "We have a soothsayer on board, my lady, and these storms can form without warning, this far out."

I'd studied enough science at university to know that storms don't materialize out of an empty sky, but I didn't say anything. Perhaps magic was involved. If that was the case, then I didn't think going belowdeck would do much good, but—

I remembered the sailors shouting the word cannon.

"It's not a storm, is it?"

The officer gazed at me with a polite and quietly desperate expression. "I really must insist you go down below, my lady."

I hadn't felt anything since I'd left the port at Arkuz, watching Father disappear into a point as we sailed away, and I didn't feel anything now. I stood up and tucked my book under my arm. The wind smelled of the ocean, not of rain, but I was aware of a flurry of activity in the masts overhead. Shouts of profanity and fear and protection charms.

"Fine," I said.

I went down below. Father had arranged for a private cabin, the last gift he ever gave me. It was large enough that if I lay flat on my back my feet would touch one end and the top of my head the other, but right now it felt claustrophobic and dark despite the magic-cast lantern swinging in the corner. I pulled out my trunk and rifled through its belongings, looking for something that might work as a weapon. The closest I found was a decorative hairpin, a long silver spike topped with jeweled flowers. She had given it to me, a sign that she knew who I really was, a sign that she was officially in on the joke. Some joke, that got me kicked out of my homeland.

I shoved my trunk back into place, pulled down my cot, and stretched out on my back, holding the hairpin to my chest.

And waited.

The ship rocked along, as calm as always. Occasionally feet pounded overhead, and the lantern would flare and then sputter —magic working its way through the walls.

I wrapped my fingers more tightly around the hairpin, the jewels digging into my palm. I closed my eyes, whispered her name.

Silence.

Silence.

Silence.

And then:

A loud, cracking boom.

I sat up as the boat jerked and tilted. My head slammed against the wall. Spots of light flared everywhere. The hairpin clattered to the ground, and I cried out and launched myself at the floor, feeling around for it in the murky shadows. The lantern was almost completely depleted.

Another round of cannon fire. The ship didn't move this time. My fingers closed in on the pin, and I brought it up just as the lantern failed.

Footsteps: pounding, frantic. Men screaming. Pistol shots. I sat hyperventilating in the dark, holding onto the hairpin as if it were her hand.

Cannon fire reverberated up from the floorboards. But the boat didn't jerk and shudder. We weren't hit.

The door to my cabin flew open.

I screamed, cowered back on my cot. A man stood in the doorway, a magic-cast lantern in one hand and a sword in the other.

"Oh shut up." He stepped inside and kicked the door closed. With his sword, he knocked down the original lantern and hung his in its place. The light was different, greenish-blue instead of white.

I shoved myself up into the corner. "Take what you want!" I shouted, kicking at my trunk. "You can have it all!" That wasn't entirely true; I'd claw his eyes out before I let him have the hairpin.

He laughed. "That ain't why we're here." The light in the lantern brightened momentarily, and I got my first good look at him: He was tall, bony, and Jokjani, although he wore a ragged Empire jacket. He paced around the cabin as he talked, his sword out, his hand on the butt of his pistol. "Just looking to take the boat. Old one don't meet with the captain's needs."

The cannon fire had stopped.

"Are you going to kill me?"

"What?" The pirate stopped. "Kill you? No, not unless you do something stupid. Captain don't like killing non-Confederates. That's you, sweetheart."

I'd read enough pirate stories to know what the Confederation was. I glared at him, which just made him laugh again.

"We'll drop you off first port we come to. Starlight Rock, most like. "

"Is that in the Empire?"

The pirate looked at me for a moment and then burst into laughter. "No, girl, it ain't in the Empire. Pirates' island, and not much there but starlight and rocks. Hence the name." He gave a little flourish as he said that last part, but my body felt like it'd been emptied out. Some abandoned pirates' island was even worse than landing in Lisirra. It was a true prison.

"You'll stay locked up in your cabins till then. Sailors got a choice of joining up or not, course. Now, if one of 'em says no—" The pirate drew a line across his throat. "Well, we drown 'em, usually, but—"

"Why are you in my room?" I didn't want to hear any more about murdering sailors.

The pirate grinned. "To keep you secure till things get settled. Ain't gonna touch you, if that's what you're worried about."

I shuddered and drew my knees up to my chest. I didn't let go of the hairpin. The pirate tapped his sword against the side of my trunk. He looked bored.

"How long's that going to take?" I said.

"Don't go planning anything." He looked at me. "I told you, we're gonna let you go."

"On a pirates' island."

"Better than the middle of the ocean."

He was right, of course. I couldn't imagine them just letting us go, but it also seemed like if this pirate was to kill me, he would have done it already.

"Couple hours," he said.

"What?"

"How long it's gonna take." He shrugged. "Till we got the new crew sorted. And then we'll be on our way."

He looked up at me and grinned, his face splitting into two, and the green light carved his face into shadows.

Continued in *The Manticore's Vow* by Cassandra Rose Clarke
Now available for purchase

EXCERPT: TWELVE: POEMS INSPIRED BY THE BROTHERS GRIMM FAIRY TALE

THE THIRD SISTER

by Andrea Blythe

The library beckoned, and she answered the call, slipping herself in between the welcoming shelves, letting the stillness and quiet seep into her, the soft motes of dust alighting on her skin and the smell of the leather-bound volumes soothing the aches of her body and spirit.

The books whispered their longing to be read. She plucked them from the shelves at random, gathering them up and cradling them in her arms. She laid them out upon a table and savored the creak of their spines as they opened.

She read—words unveiling worlds more astounding than the glittering gold and silver gardens she and her sisters found hidden under their floorboards. She read until the candles burned low, until her eyes felt like sand and her vision blurred, until her spine bent into a bow, and she fell into a restful sleep, a treatise on the alchymical uses of plants as a pillow.

As time passed, she faded into the library more and more

—so many hours at a stretch, the days and nights blurred together in a litany of poetry and candlelight. She read and she wrote, the nib of her plume scratching out the results of her research, ink-splotched pages filled so thickly with text they appeared black. When visiting students and scholars spoke with her, she held discourse on the natural world and the worlds beyond, leaving them wide-eyed and awed when they returned to their universities.

Her father sent messengers to draw her back into the sitting rooms and gardens and ballrooms, the light and airy places where princesses belonged. When this failed, he stormed into the library himself, prepared to drive her out with the thunder of his speech and the lightning of his hand. The tall stone shelves greeted him with their towering height —full of tomes of natural history and philosophy and mathematics alongside the ramblings of novelists and the fancies of poets—all the crushing weight of knowledge pressing down upon him. He searched and found only books and silence, the whisper of his own breath loud in his ears. Eventually, the eerie quiet unsettled and drove him back to the clattering noise of the court, to the voices and laughter and music that filled up his thoughts and hours.

The library became her realm. She slept on the nests of old discarded pamphlets and nourished herself on the pages she consumed. Over time, her skin paled and hair thinned. Her hands became marked with paper cuts, nails black with ink. She padded through the shelves like a specter, leaving a wake of near-completed tracts and treatises and historical accounts at her feet—treasures scholars discovered and smuggled out into the world, published anonymously to great acclaim and outrage. She was rarely seen, more mythic creature than person—a ghost some said, a monster, a patron saint of the stacks. It was a blessing, it was said, or a curse, claimed others, to see her and have her look upon you. She might read you and find in your flesh the story that shapes you.

Continued in Twelve by Andrea Blythe
Forthcoming in Fall 2020

EXCERPT: LOCAL STAR

By Aimee Ogden

There was nowhere Triz Cierrond would rather be than elbows-deep in a starfighter. But twenty levels above her, the Hab's main arcade was crammed with people celebrating the victorious return of the Confederated Fleet. For once in her life, the station wrenchworks were the last place she wanted to be.

And Kalo was the last person she wanted to be stuck there with.

It was partly her fault, for making him wait while she finished checking in the other six light attack Swarmers. But if she had to be miserable, her ex might as well be too. S*oon,* soon, she'd be uphab celebrating with Casne and her quadparents. A small part of her knew she was hesitating over that too. Probably best to wait a few hours anyway, to give them some time to try being one big happy family. She still didn't know how she fit into that equation.

Triz ducked under the left-hand engine pod of Kalo's swarmer, noting an oozing coolant leak where the wing had partially sheared away from the fuselage. Scorch marks streaked the cockpit, and the nosecone was less of a cone now than an impact-flattened nub. She shook her head and recorded a note on the tab*let: total wrench* job. "Shitting stars," she muttered, and pulled her facemask up over her nose and mouth. "How are you not dead after this?"

"I apologize on behalf of the Cyberbionautic Alliance. I'm sure the ceebees wish they'd finished the job almost as much as you do." Kalo sprawled atop Triz's eternally-in-progress refit of an Escoth V-27 engine assembly. The Escoth, as well as the pile of damaged ore-Scoopers hurriedly rearranged behind it, had been set aside for the sudden influx of paying work. Ships like Escoths were fast and sporty, great for fixing up and selling for a little credit. The Scoopers were scavenger crafts that filtered through the silt layers on the outside of asteroids, panning for something richer than iron oxide in that dust. Kalo didn't seem to mind his precarious position. If the prospect of getting oil on his dress greens alarmed him, he didn't show it. He didn't look at her, but combed one hand through wavy, dark hair. He needed a haircut.

Not that it mattered much how he looked. Once he escaped to the festivities uphab, he and anyone else in a Fleet uniform would be deluged by offers of drinks and dalliances tonight, and those with a Light Attack Swarm pin on their collar more than most. Greaseball mechanics just didn't invite the same level of attention—especially the ones who'd grown up as guttergirls in a recycling engine, and with the manners to match.

Casne would probably be just as beset with admirers as Kalo . . . but Triz knew her best friend and most significant of others wouldn't be entertaining outside interest tonight. Some things were worth waiting for. Triz dragged her stylus across the screen of her tablet, scratching out her notes one slow stroke at a time. She glanced over at Kalo, who was fidgeting with one of his silver-ringed cuffs. Good. Let him be impatient.

"I was thinking," said Kalo, and Triz's stylus froze against the screen. There were a lot of things that could come after those three words, and she doubted any of them would improve the current situation. "The atmospheric handling hasn't been great for me lately. The greaseheads over at Auzhni Hab got a little creative with the repairs after that little to-do outside Hedgehome, and it's not exactly sticking on a hard turn, but it's *not exactly* not, either. If you could just get in there and change the calibration of the—"

"Don't tell me how to do my job." That did it. She scratched off the rest of the note in shorthand, signed it, and stormed across the wrenchworks bay to thrust the tablet at Kalo. "It'll take me forever to get this thing spaceworthy. How long is the Fleet here?" Longer meant more time with Casne; it also meant more chances for head-to-head collisions with Kalo and the shrapnel of their former relationship.

It was supposed to be fun. Kalo was supposed to be fun.

Until he'd neatly snipped things off right before the Fleet left for Hedgehome: no reasons, just a polite this-isn't-working-is-it, just shy of nine cycles after Casne had enthusiastically introduced them—almost a whole year together, reckoning by the local star! But no great surprise there: they'd been skimming that event horizon for a while already. Triz had found herself starting idle fights whenever Kalo was back on-Hab, finding annoyances in little things that hadn't bothered her before. Just as well, because gods, was it annoying to ask someone to give a shit about you as they flew blithely off to their untimely death! At least Casne crewed a whaleship, one of those practically Hab-sized behemoths with just enough engines attached to nudge them through space. Whaleships were built to withstand fire, cradling their heavy-fire tactical arrays, providing a safe haven for their battered swarms to return to after battle. Whaleships always came home . . . almost always. With Light Attack

Swarms, the odds weren't so good. And when they did come home, it might well be in pieces of a size suitable for packing in a mealcase.

He'd left her. And now he was back here, in her 'works. Trying to be friendly.

If Kalo noticed her taut silence while scanning through her notes, he didn't reach out to strum it. He scrolled upward several times to get through her full report, and he whistled low when he reached the end. "Gods of Issam. I really should be dead."

"Better luck next time." She poked his hand that held the stylus, and he dashed off a signature. The tablet chirped politely, and an invoice estimate winged its way to the Fleet bursary at Centerpoint. "Maybe next time, don't burn so hard on a wing when you know it's busted."

"Don't tell me how to do my job." Kalo tossed the tablet back to her and she caught it low, just a few inches above the ground. "Thanks for the lookover. The Fleet's parked here for three days while we refuel and wait for Centerpoint to stop shitting their pants over what to do with the ceebees and actually send us our new orders. If you don't have the time to fix me up altogether, at least get things started so the techs on the whaleship don't have to start from scratch." His mouth twisted in that familiar half-smile she couldn't help but love to hate. "Or if you're short on time, you can skip making it spaceworthy and just set up a feedback loop in the coolant line so I blow up halfway between here and Centerpoint. That'll save both you and the techs a lot of trouble."

"I wouldn't." Dragging a clearance hose, she retreated back under the Swarmer, as much to put some space between them as to start working. "Casne would know it was me and I'd never hear the end of it."

He followed her over to the repair bay and leaned against the good wing with one arm. "Well, I certainly wouldn't want my murder to cause you any inconvenience. Besides, you'd miss me if I was space dust."

The hose was heavy; Triz bent her knees to get under it and tried not to look like she was struggling. He might do something really hideous, like offer to help. "The only way I'd miss you is with a lancet gun. And not more than once."

He ducked his head under the fuselage. "And yet here we are, alone in the wrenchworks. By your plan, by the way, not mine. Not that I'm objecting. If there's anything you wanted to say—"

The metallorganic seal on the hose suctioned itself onto the gaping wound in the side of Kalo's Swarmer, and Triz flipped the switch on the pump with her foot. The vacuum clattered twice then roared to life, slurping down the coolant spillage and its unwanted fumes. "We're all set here," Triz shouted over the noisy belching of the pump. She wasn't sure if Kalo could hear her over the noise and didn't especially care. The vacuum spoke for itself.

He yelled something back at her and gestured to the pair of lifts that stretched all the way through the Hab. The wrenchworks made up the bottom of the station—or at least what everyone agreed via the consensus of artificial gravity counted as "bottom," in deep space—the lift started here, then crossed the recycling and recovery levels, the living quarters, and the arcade, ending in Justice at the very top. Maybe he was asking where to go now? Triz couldn't pick just one of the seven hells, so she shrugged and slipped her earmuffs from around her neck to cover her ears. Finally, Kalo gave up and disappeared into one of the lifts.

Triz gave it two minutes to make sure he was really gone, then killed the vacuum and collapsed against the battered Swarmer. Intellectually, she knew the fighting between the ceebees and the Confederated Fleet had been ugly. She'd seen the vids of dead alien intelligences after the ceebee commander's attempts at rapidfire terraforming: lifeless mounds of iridescent tendrils and broken segments of carapace, poisoned by the introduction of atmospheric oxygen. Sitting beside the newsport, she'd listened to the rolls of names of planetary colonists killed in the forcible resettlements at Hedgehome. Ceebees never balked at remaking their own bodies, using any and every tech available to fit themselves to their environment; they'd proven they had equally few qualms about remaking an environment to better serve them to often horrific effect.

It was strange now, to have the war brought to her own door like this. Usually, the wrenchworks here at her home habitation ring of Vivik didn't see more than the odd freighter every week or two. Vivik's local star had no habitable planets and nothing particular to recommend it beyond a gas giant resort for platform jumpers. Even its economic role as a shipping-lane nexus for the past hundred years only allowed freight to pass through on its way to the bigger systems farther out.

Triz liked Vivik Hab's usual quiet. Her home for the past ten years had always offered her safety.

But Moxu and Vogett, the two closest big Habs on this ragged edge of settled space, had been destroyed in the fighting, leaving Vivik the only nearby survivor able to pick up the pieces of the Fleet and send it on toward the center of the Galactic Web. Ships weren't the only wreckage clotting the Hab. None other than Commander Rocan shitting Dustald-3 Melviq himself was a prisoner of Justice here. Many of Vivik's citizens had already gone to war; now war had come to the Hab itself, too.

When she could breathe again, she emerged from under the Swarmer's belly and hurried into the wrenchworks office. The earmuffs clanged when she tossed them into her locker, and she scanned her wristfob for a tiny water ration to splash her face in the sink. She didn't want to open the fighter up until she was sure it was coolant-free, so no reason not to celebrate with the rest of the Hab. She could buy a round for some friendly-looking whaleship crews and still give Casne time and space to enjoy her quadparents for a while yet.

No time to bother with changing into something fancier; Triz ducked out of the office and fussed briefly with her hair. She wondered if she'd be able to find any of Casne's Fleet friends to follow around for the night. If nothing else she might be able to find them on the outskirts of the crowd of admirers the favored Captain Casne Vivik Veling had surely collected by now. They could hit Ganit's Pantry, and hopefully Ganit hadn't jacked up the price of boot gin by three hundred percent for the night—

The lift flashed an alert: visitors incoming. Damn Kalo. What, did he decide to give it one more go for old time's sake? Her heart lurched. But then a comfortably familiar scowl settled into her face, and she folded her arms.

The lift doors parted, and Triz choked on the deep breath she'd held. Casne exploded out of the lift and picked her up in a hug. Triz's arms locked around Casne's back, and she gasped down a deep breath to keep from bursting into sudden, silly tears. Casne's tight curls carried the faint electric smell of the interior of a whaleship, but she still smelled like home to Triz.

After several long moments that would never be quite long enough, Casne pulled back. "All right, greasemark," she shouted over the vacuum's roaring and laid a warm kiss on Triz's lower lip. "Are you going to buy me a drink, or what?"

Continued in Local Star by Aimee Ogden
Forthcoming in 2020 from Interstellar Flight Press

EDITORS & CONTRIBUTORS

Erin Becker is a freelance writer and MFA candidate at Vermont College of Fine Arts. She lives in the south of Chile, where she runs a small communications and translation business. She's written reviews for *MAKE Lit + Luz* and *Lambda Literary* and is interested in all things forward-thinking and feminist.

Andrea Blythe bides her time waiting for the apocalypse by writing speculative poetry and fiction. She is the author of *Your Molten Heart / A Seed to Hatch* (2018) a collection of erasure poems created from the pages of Trader Joe's Fearless Flyers, and coauthor of *Every Girl Becomes the Wolf* (*Finishing Line Press*, 2018), a collaborative chapbook written with Laura Madeline Wiseman. She is a cohost of the New Books in Poetry podcast and is a member of the Science Fiction and Fantasy Poetry Association and the Horror Writers Association. Find her online at www.andreablythe.com, on Twitter @andreablythe, and on Instagram @andreablythe.

Jeremy Brett is an Associate Professor at Texas A&M University. At Texas A&M's Cushing Memorial Library & Archives, he is the Processing Archivist as well as the Curator of the Science Fiction & Fantasy Research Collection, one of the world's largest of its kind. He received his M.L.S. and his M.A. (History) from the University of Maryland, College Park.

Cassandra Rose Clarke's novels have been finalists for the Philip K. Dick Award, the Romantic Times Reviewer's Choice Award, and YALSA's Best Fiction for Young Adults. Her poetry has placed second in the Rhysling Awards, been nominated for the Pushcart Prize, and appeared in *Strange Horizons, Star*Line*, and elsewhere. Cassandra graduated in 2006 from The University of St. Thomas with a B.A. in English, and two years later she completed her master's degree in creative writing at The University of Texas at Austin. In 2010 she attended the Clarion West Writer's Workshop in Seattle, where she was a recipient of the Susan C. Petrey Clarion Scholarship Fund. She is currently the associate director for a Houston-based literary arts nonprofit, Writespace.

Kaylee Craig is the author of *emotion-time continuum*, an experimental free-verse poetry book jam-packed with poetry on a variety of personal and social topics, and *All in a Seed* (2019), a poetry chapbook that reflects on lessons of growth and healing that are inspired by nature. Kaylee also has works featured in *Drunk Monkeys, Medium*, and *Thought Catalog*. She enjoys writing magical realism and science fiction, poetry, and nonfiction about mental health, lifestyle, and society.

Michael Glazner's writing has appeared in *Literally Stories, After the Pause*, and the daily newspaper of Tutrakan, Bulgaria. Southwestern University awarded him a B.A. in Communication, and he teaches high school English in the Houston area. When not reading, writing, or editing genre fiction, he enjoys time spent with his dogs and strong cups of coffee.

Piper J. Daniels is a Michigan native and queer intersectional feminist currently living in the American Southwest. Her debut essay collection, *Ladies Lazarus*, won the Tarpaulin Sky Book Award, was longlisted for the PEN Diamonstein-Spielvogel Award for the Art of the Essay, and was named a finalist for the Lambda Literary Award in LGBTQ Nonfiction. She is the founder of a manuscript consultation collective that serves POC and LGBTQ writers.

Archita Mittra is a writer and artist with a love for all things vintage, gothic and darkly fantastical. A feminist, pop-culture geek, and sometimes gamer, she lives in Calcutta (India) with her family, rabbits, and a library of books she hopes to finish in the next life. You can follow her on Twitter and Instagram @architamittra and find out more about her work at archita.666@gmail.com.

J.T. Morse is a multi-genre writer/editor/photographer with a love of character-driven narratives and hybrid works. She likes to dig deep, find the magic in the mundane, and pry open doors with her wordsmithing super skills. Connection is her 'why' for life and creating. Morse's work has been published by *Balance of Seven Press, Texas Living Magazine, Paragraph Planet, Central Coast Poetry Show, Haiku Journal, Nightmare Press, Art Houston Magazine,* and other publications. She's a facilitator/instructor at Writespace Houston and is frequently a featured panelist/presenter at a variety of literary festivals and cons. Most of Morse's work is penned in her garden balcony, perched high above her mystical ranch in the Piney Woods of Texas, where she lives with her husband, daughter, and twenty-three spoiled-rotten rescue animals. Her website is perpetually in a state of flux, but you should be able to find out more about her at www.jtmorsewriter.com, if the wind blows just right and the internet ghosts are feeling frisky.

Aimee Ogden is a former science teacher and software tester; now she writes stories about sad astronauts, angry princesses, and dead gods. Her short fiction has appeared in venues such as *Analog, Beneath Ceaseless Skies*, and *Fireside*, and another novella, *Sun-daughters, Sea-daughters* is forthcoming from Tor.com. She also co-edits *Translunar Travelers Lounge*, a magazine of fun and optimistic speculative fiction.

Caitlin Starling is a writer and spreadsheet-wrangler who lives near Portland, Oregon. Equipped with an anthropology degree and an unhealthy interest in the dark and macabre, she writes horror-tinged speculative fiction of all flavors. Her first novel, *The Luminous Dead*, is nominated for the Bram Stoker Award for Superior Achievement in a First Novel. She has two gothic horror tales forthcoming: *Yellow Jessamine* (novella, *Neon Hemlock* 2020) and *The Death of Jane Lawrence* (novel, St Martin's Press 2021), as well as a novella in the upcoming *Vampire: The Masquerade* audio collection, *Walk Among Us*. Caitlin also works in narrative design for interactive theater and games, and has been paid to design body parts. She's always on the lookout for new ways to inflict insomnia.

Presley Thomas is a writer and teacher in Houston, TX. His work has appeared in Interstellar Flight Press and New Body.

John Tuttle is a Catholic man from a small town in Illinois who has a passion for truth and beauty. A journalist as well as a creative, he has functioned as a judge for several *Ageless Authors* anthologies. His short fiction has been published by *Zombie Pirate Publishing*, and he has had articles published by *Midwest Film Journal, The University Bookman, The Hill*, and the University of Notre Dame's *Grotto Network*. His photography has been featured by *Blue Marble Review* and *The William and Mary Review*. His short film "The Amazing World of Insects" won first place in the youth category of the 2017 SkeenaWild Film Fest.

E.D. Walker, a native of Los Angeles, is the author of *The Fairy Tales of Lyond Series* that begins with *Enchanting the King*. E.D.'s short fiction has appeared in the *USA Today* best-selling anthologies *Pets in Space* 3 and *Pets in Space 4*. You can find her online at www.edwalkerauthor.com and on Twitter @AuthorEDW.

T.D. Walker is the author of *Small Waiting Objects* (*CW Books*, 2019). Her poems and stories have appeared in *Strange Horizons, Web Conjunctions, The Cascadia Subduction Zone, Luna Station Quarterly,* and elsewhere. She draws on both her grounding in literary studies and her experience as a computer programmer in writing her poetry and fiction.

Holly Lyn Walrath is a freelance editor and author based out of Houston, Texas. She holds a B.A. in English from The University of Texas and a Master's in Creative Writing from the University of Denver. Her poetry and short fiction has appeared in *Strange Horizons, Fireside Fiction, Daily Science Fiction, Luna Station Quarterly, Liminality, a*nd elsewhere. She is the author of the Elgin Award winning chapbook *Glimmerglass Girl* (*Finishing Line Press*, 2018) and her chapbook in Italian, *Numinose Lapidi* (*Kipple Press*, 2020). In Houston, she collaborates with Writespace, Comicpalooza, writers, artists, and creative communities to make the writing world a more fantastical place.

Kade Walton is an author and devotee of all things SFF. They hold a B.S. in Political Science and put it to work in twisted ways by writing speculative fiction and analyzing huge amounts of media across genres. They're also a food justice advocate and creator of the forthcoming indie serial *Ain't No Way Back Home*. They live in the mountains of Western North Carolina with their partner and overflowing vegetable garden.

INTERSTELLAR FLIGHT PRESS

Interstellar Flight Press is an indie speculative publishing house. We feature innovative works from the best new writers in science fiction and fantasy. In the words of Ursula K. Le Guin, we need "writers who can see alternatives to how we live now, can see through our fear-stricken society and its obsessive technologies to other ways of being, and even imagine real grounds for hope."

Find us online at www.interstellarflightpress.com.

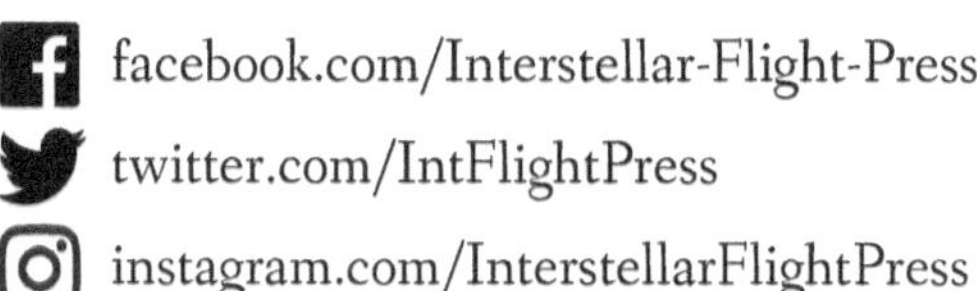

www.ingramcontent.com/pod-product-compliance
Lightning Source LLC
Chambersburg PA
CBHW030751110726
47900CB00008B/2558

* 9 7 8 1 7 3 3 8 8 6 2 6 0 *